The Sea in My Blood

The Sea in My Blood

by

William Finch

Published by:
NOSTALGIA PUBLICATIONS
(Terry Davy)
7 Elm Park, Toftwood,
Dereham, Norfolk
NR19 1NB

First impression: 1992
Reprinted: 1998

ISBN 0 947630 24 4

Originally published as ISBN 0 9520075 0 9
by William Finch

Design and typesetting by:
TERRY DAVY

Printed by:
PAGE BROS. (NORWICH) LTD.
Mile Cross Lane,
Norwich,
Norfolk NR6 6SA

Front cover illustration:
Smack at Sea

Back cover illustration:
Morning after Boxing Day

(both by the author)

The Great Unknown

I dedicate "The Sea in My Blood" to my wife, with love and in gratitude for her support and forbearance.

Contents

Foreword

"The Sea in My Blood" is my tribute to Father and all Lowestoft smacksmen and their ships. It is not a history.

It is based largely on my memory which has confidently taken me back beyond my fourth birthday. A number of retired smacksmen have written to me. I have had fascinating and very informative chats with others. Regrettably only very few are left.

I thank them for their help and their encouragement.

The illustrations are my own. Most were done at the time. A few are developed from my other contemporary rough sketches.

I knew intimately the men and their ships. I have long felt the compulsion to write this book. First, because of my admiration for smacks and smacksmen, both outstanding in our maritime story. Second, because I hope it will bring them to the notice of the widest of readerships, with the confidence that they will share my interest and affection. Third, because they are in imminent danger of being forgotten – even by Lowestoft, to whom they brought many years of prosperity.

W. R. Finch

Looking down at Crimson Rose

Chapter 1

In The Beginning

It had been a long walk to the harbour for a nine year old. I now stood on the edge of the quayside, miserable and not a little scared. I looked down at the fishing smack, Crimson Rose, my home for the next few days. She was the first I had seen at close quarters. She was the first I ever boarded. It was the first time I had been to Lowestoft harbour.

It looked so scaringly far down to that narrow strip of filthy green, slimy and debris splattered

without tripping over something or falling down one of those holes? I was soon to go with him!

My doubts began soon after we left home. This was all my own fault! A fact which gave me no com-fort. How I argued with both mother and father. How strong minded – or stubborn they were – we all were!

"No", said father when I asked, "Can I come with you on your next trip?" (voyage was never used). His "No" always implied "and no arguments". "No good trying to get your father to change his mind", Mother said, often. She, too, was strong minded – or stubborn! Yet the mystery still remains, how did I persuade her to allow one of her little Finches to fly away into the unknown? I can only make a few suggestions.

Dangerous Chaos?

water between her and the quayside. Soon, by some means or other, I had to clear that gap.

I looked at Crimson Rose – and wondered. Such a muddle of wood, rope and netting cluttered a large part of her deck, which itself was dotted with obstacles and dark openings. These and the two masts with furled sails and different kinds of rope all over the place. How could father dare to go to sea? How, when he got there, did he move about

One comes immediately. I, too, am strong minded – stubborn. Did they finally agree out of sheer desperation? Another closely follows. Did they feel they were on to a certain bet when I accepted the proviso to their "yes". "You will be up and ready at six o'clock tomorrow morning!" I was by far the worst "getter up" in the whole family. I gobbled many a breakfast and often chewed my way to school – I am sure that father saw himself

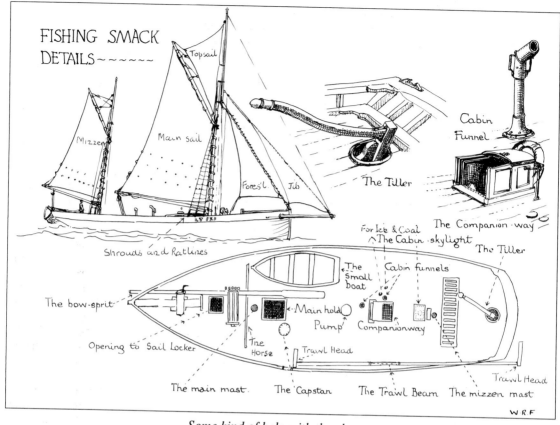

FISHING SMACK
DETAILS ~ ~ ~ ~ ~

Topsail

Mizzen

Main sail

Fores'l   Jib

Shrouds and Ratlines

The Tiller

Cabin Funnel

The Companion way

For Ice & Coal
The Cabin skylight

The Tiller

Cabin funnels

The Small boat

The bow-sprit

Main hold
Pump

Companionway

Opening to Sail Locker

The Horse

Trawl Head

The main mast.   The 'Capstan   The Trawl Beam   The mizzen mast

Trawl Head

W R F

Some kind of help with the chaos

leaving home at six the next morning an unimpeded and relieved man.

I went to bed, as determined as ever, and created a mental clock. I can still see it with it's hands

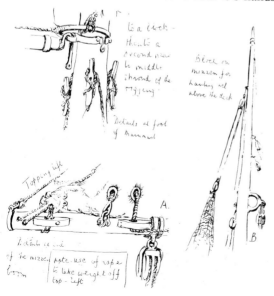

Adding to my chaos!

pointing to just before six. It was the last thing I remember before falling asleep and the first I saw when I woke up.

So with a rather crestfallen father, and leaving a worried mother, I left for something as distant and mysterious as the moon – to me.

A third suggestion, and the one which has given my title, "The Sea in my Blood", gains in strength and substance even as I write. Both mother and father had strongly sea coloured pedigrees, which clearly passed more strongly to me than to my six brothers and sisters or to my numerous cousins except, perhaps, one – and he is only in a nuclear submarine! Did like appeal to like? Was there possibly a touch of paternal pride – was I at 9 a chip off the old block?

I wonder, in the depth of his exasperation with me, did a tiny flicker of memory remind him, "I did this once!"?

Round about twelve he ran away to become a smacksman. His Something was strong enough – and courageous enough – to ignore a very strict, rather awesome father. His first attempt failed, because, unwisely, he took with him his younger brother, Uncle Jimmy, "a bit of a lad". On their way

Jimmy could not resist "getting his own back" on an unpopular neighbour by tying an empty can to the leg of his goose. The resulting noise, as it clattered down the narrow, cemented alley way, aroused a lot of irate people, among them Grandfather. After a stiff dose of his belt, leather, they spent the rest of that day and all the next in the bedroom on bread and water.

His second venture, by himself, succeeded. Grandfather did nothing. "Let the young fool learn for himself". He did, fifty years later. "Anybody who speaks of the romance of the sea", he decided, "Should have his head examined".

Whether or not my Something had any effect on the argument I cannot prove, but I can present strong evidence of it's presence in me – almost at birth!

I am blessed with a very good and reliable memory. This I can prove.

I plainly remember a feeling of betrayal when mother left me on the morning of my first day at school in Oulton Broad. This was before my fifth birthday. "I was advanced for my age" they said. Granny Macey, whom we called Mums, said, "He's always pestering with his questions"

We Finches and Macey's formed a kind of sea and ship settlement in Carleton Colville. We lived in the end house and in the same terrace were mother's parents, Grandfather Macey and Mums, also Granny Finch, father's mother, and one daughter and six sons.

Not far away lived another Finch, Uncle Albert, a master ship–wright. Aunt Sarah, father's one sister, was our kind of roving reporter who kept us in touch with the ordinary world.

Behind our house lay a wide expanse of scrubland which seemed to belong to nobody. It ended at the edge of a wide stretch of water linking Oulton to the Broads and to Lowestoft. It was always busy with shipping and on the far bank men dealt with the sea in the ship yards.

Well beyond Uncle Albert's I could just see a higgledy, piggledy mass of masts and funnels, "Its where ships go to die", they told me.

Much nearer, and well within my walking distance, was a timbered quay to which Norfolk wherries moored to unload lime. I can still remember describing to mother their tiny cabins, "They have everything, even a tiny stove – and black and white lino on the floor!" I well remember with my friend Jackie Rounce, whose dad owned the quay, exploring those lovely ships and freeing the mooring rope of one. Scared, we ran home. Fortunately father was there. He quickly dealt with it – and me.

Father came home briefly and disappeared to sea for much longer. Uncle Bob and Uncle Jimmy did the same. Uncle Albert, the master craftsman,

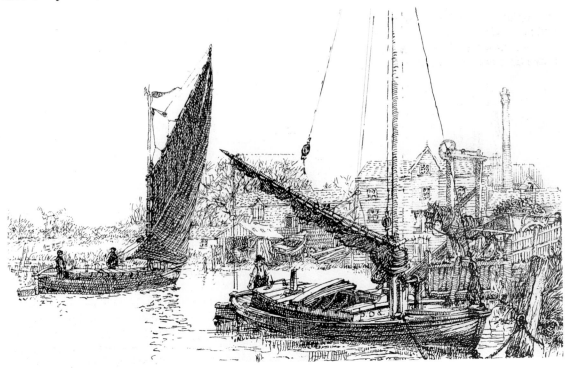

Wherry Memories

11

and Uncle Herbert, apprentice ship–wright – for five long years! – went daily, including every Saturday morning, to build and repair ships.

So my tender Oulton Broad years nurtured my Something, "The Sea in my Blood".

It responded very quickly when Aunt Sarah remarked to mother, "I hear Billy's lying on the hard". Billy was my father. The "hard" flashed into my mind as a rough, shingly beach and, for some mysterious reason, brought with it a picture of his smack – I had never yet seen one, except dimly and distantly from Lowestoft beach. My completed

question she said, "To daddy. He's away at the west'd". Satisfied because I knew – how did I know? – that daddy had gone a long way away to fish I decided to "write". She gave me pencil and I "wrote". I found an envelope, used, and unbeknown to mother –there was danger from a passing cart, or cyclist! – I slipped across the road to post it – with difficulty, because I could not quite reach the slot. So I tipped it in. "I'm afraid he won't get your letter", mother said, "The postman won't be able to read your scribble". So I had not yet begun schooling – which I did before I was five.

Longshore Boats

mental picture showed a smack looming dark and large in the night, hauled up on a stony stretch, with father lying sound asleep by it's side. I felt so sorry for him, because he was wrapped only in a thin blanket.

The Hard was, as I learned years afterwards, a stony strip bordering Lowestoft harbour, upon which, in bad times to save the cost of the dry dock or a slipway, they keeled their smacks for repairing and cleaning.

My Something responded as clearly when I saw mother writing a letter. In reply to the inevitable

From the early months of the year to round about the beginning of summer Lowestoft fishermen went to "Th' West'd", to Devon and Cornwall, especially to Brixham, Newlyn and Padstow, for the much better fishing.

Indisputably still at Oulton Broad, because I can clearly see myself climbing on to the large kitchen table by way of a big, upturned bucket, one of two regularly filled at the well, quite a walk away. My aim was to cover an expanse of the back of a stretch of wallpaper, which overlapped the top, with a drawing. The subject – a sailing ship. I can also see myself thus risking my "Sunday Best" – a sailor suit, complete with a wide brimmed straw hat with a ribbon, saying "H.M.S. Something or Other". We were due to visit relatives in Lowestoft – over five miles there and back! "Would you like me to show you how Grandfather draws seagulls?", mother said. He was a very accomplished artist. Lowestoft chose one of his very large oil paintings for a fisheries exhibition in London. It's subject – "The Lowestoft Smack's Regatta"!

I can see mother's face when she saw my masterpiece. "Oh Billy", she exclaimed, "You've ruined it!" Only tiny patches of my ship peered through the few gaps left by the largest flock of gulls – ever.

My grandparents undoubtedly stimulated and fed my Something with their stories of my forbears closely linked with the sea. Granny Finch was a mine of information on Royalty and the Aristocracy, their ancestry, births, deaths, marriages, their possessions and wealth, and even tinges of scandal. Not that I encouraged her, but, "Once let her begin" mother said "There's no stopping her". Fortunately, for me, this was also true when she regaled me with stories of my Devonian ancestors, shipbuilders, ship owners, sea captains, seamen, smugglers – and perhaps – even a pirate. One, a smuggler, profited. He bought land and property, but "the customs found him out and took everything". She told me the tragic story of Grandfather Finch.

He owned his vessel, a long–shore boat licensed only to fish within a mile or so from the coast. On a quiet sunny day in high summer, with holiday makers thronging the south pier which formed the south part of the harbour mouth, he made for home. As he was about to enter the quieter water, a sharp squall struck and capsized his boat. The horrified holidaymakers saw both men, Uncle Teddy, his youngest son, was with him, trapped under the ship's one great sail. Grandfather's body was never found. Weeks later the other one surfaced identifiable only by a garnsey. That belonged to Uncle Bob his older brother so the paper reported Bob's death – giving an unpleasant twist to the tragedy. Uncle Teddy, wearing Uncle Bob's garnsey, took his place because Bob had complained of a bad cold that morning.

They appear on the long list of those lost at sea on the memorial in the Lowestoft parish church of St. Margaret.

Grandfather and Uncle Teddy stared down at me from the opposite wall as I sat on Granny's prickly horse hair sofa, the back of my knees becoming sorer and sorer. The muzzy, fuzziness of the vignetted photographic style of those days formed clouds around each head and made me decide they had already got to heaven!

As Granny talked and talked, she knitted and knitted, her steel needles clicked and clicked. She occasionally glanced at her work which, from large balls of off–white, greasy wool called "ob", she produced the fishermen's long thick, sea–boat stockings.

Of father's brothers Uncle Bob and Uncle Jimmy went to sea. I considered them inferior to father as a fisherman, "they only worked in drifters", (herring boats).

The sea with personalities and stories came as strongly from mother and her parents. They told of those who built, owned, and sailed ships to all parts of the world. They told fascinating stories of dangers at sea. One of my favourites included an unsolved mystery, perhaps of murder, and of a fortune unobtainable.

Grandfather Macey had been a prosperous Billingsgate fish merchant and a smack owner. He transferred to Lowestoft at the time of great development in the fishing industry brought by the arrival of the Great Eastern Railway. Granny Macey claimed he was one of the founders of the town's growth to a leading fishing port. When I knew him he had nothing. "He was neither a drunkard nor a bad businessman", Granny said, "but one whisky made him a 'soft touch', and, if only half the people who owed him money would pay him back we would be well off". So when I knew them they lived in poverty.

He had stories of ships and the sea and he told them well and illustrated one with a sketch. This one began:

"I went up forrard to see to the fores'l. I took hold of the winch handle – it was a big one made of iron – and I pressed down hard – I don't remember any more until I woke up in hospital with my heard covered in bandages – I could hardly see".

He described what happened.

A cog broke as he worked the handle. It flew back with such force as to throw him overboard. The skipper of a passing smack thought he was a bundle of rags! The crew launched the little boat.

I was to learn how long that took, first to clear the several odds and ends. then to haul it to the side and manhandle it over the rail and drop it into the sea. At least a quarter of an hour must have passed before they reached him. "I had a broken arm, a shattered forehead and my brains were hanging out!", he said. Yet he kept afloat! Mother said he was such a strong swimmer that he took her, as a small child, far out to sea on his back. Granny Macey now entered the story.

"At the time of the accident", she said, "I knew it was the same time because I had just looked at the clock, and at that moment something touched my forehead. It felt like a cold, wet hand". She described what happened when she first visited him in hospital. "I couldn't recognise him", she said. "His face was covered with bandages". He was still unconscious. So she sat by his bedside. "Suddenly", she said, "An extraordinary thing happened – Grandfather began to whistle "Nearer my God to thee" his favourite hymn – it was beautiful. I had never heard him whistle before!" – and – Grandfather said, "I can't whistle. I can't even whistle a dog".

He used to show me his scarred right fore–arm. I can still see the dent in his forehead, deep enough to take my small fist, and his constantly nodding head which increased as he told his stories.

Another of his sea adventures began,

"The weather was dreadful and getting worse –". This happened when he was skipper of Bella, his last smack before the crash came. They battened down everything. He sent the crew below and double lashed himself to the tiller – "Just as well", he said, "I felt something was coming".

"Suddenly", he said, "a great wave came, as tall as a house. I found myself almost looking straight up at it". It fell on Grandfather and the ship. He survived, except for a thorough dowsing, but poor Bella – snapped mainmast, split mizzen, smashed bulwarks, bits of timber, ropes, rigging, sails all over the deck and hanging over the side. Water streaming everywhere and cascading through the scuppers.

Grandfather described how "they set to". They rigged bits of sail and replaced as well they could the smashed bulwarks "The waves were still coming over the side". They rigged a jury main mast, using an oar roped to what was left of it. Grandfather explained, "We could already steer her, but now she could move along".

They turned to down below. Not too much water because of the careful battening–down, – but – no fire in both the boiler and Cooky's galley. Almost miraculously they found dry wood and paper – but – no usable matches. "Now", said Grandfather, "I remembered something said to me quite a time ago. Always take a corked bottle of matches, you never know when they'll come in handy. I rummaged in my bunk, and, there it was!" They tried several, but, they were either too damp, or just spluttered and went out. "Then", said Grandfather, "I remembered something else, if a match won't light, rub it through your hair". The first few failed, then one kept alight long enough. "That was the best mug of tea I ever tasted", he said.

The heavy weather abated and helped Bella as she sailed slowly homewards. Lowestoft was fortunately less than a day away. As she neared home a steamer offered a tow. "I didn't want it", said Grandfather, "I told him as we'd got so far we'd get back without any help". To his surprise a great crowd awaited them, "How did they know?" he asked.

Bella makes for home

After repairs Bella went back to sea, still as tough as the rest.

As I sat in their sitting room, sadly full of reminders of their one time prosperity, I saw two quite large objects one each side of the fireplace. The were authenticated mammoth bones and were exciting, not only because they were so very old, but also because Grandfather had trawled them up. So every time I saw the cod–end emptied on to the deck I hoped to see a find as exciting!

When "them there blokes in London" decided that all mates and skippers must have "a sustifficate" they chose Grandfather as both teacher and examiner. He accepted, reluctantly, and I am sure that not a few passed because of him.

They excited me with just the mention of one relative, a Captain Bartlet, master of a deep sea sailing ship – a wind–jammer no less, the kind I had tried so hard to draw – and when I learned his was the kind engaged – among them The Cutty Sark – in exciting tea and wool races to and from very far off places, I longed to meet him – but never did.

Another story of a wind–jammer, an unsolved mystery and money unobtainable, was among my favourites.

The hero, or victim, was a young midshipman, a distant relative, due to board a wind–jammer in Liverpool docks for his final training. He arrived at his hotel. He booked in. He left his luggage in his bedroom. He came down. "I won't be long", he said to the porter as he left – and disappeared. Neither the police, nor the private detective hired by Grandfather found a trace of him. Mystery then came upon mystery. The ship to which he had been assigned, she vanished too. With her went any hope of proving whether he had sailed in her – or not! Was he murdered in Liverpool, drowned at sea, or, most unlikely, just decided to disappear?

He had lots of money. Much of it should have come to us. "What has happened to it?" I asked. "It's in chancery", they said and tried to explain, with the result that to me for several years, it was a huge cupboard in which they stored all the money which people could not prove belonged to them. I proposed several schemes – one at least questionable – for getting theirs, all turned down. What a difference all that money would have made to them.

During my many chats with Grandfather Macey I mentioned things I wanted, and I remember he promised that he would help me to buy whatever it was "When my ship comes in", not "When I've got more money". I visualised this ship as a magnificent yacht such as visited Lowestoft each summer. I once almost dragged him to the yacht harbour because I had seen such a ship, "and it could be yours!" Unfortunately his never came in. They died penniless.

Throughout my very early years in Oulton Broad father was a shadowy but impressive figure who stayed for a very short time with us but was away at sea for much longer. Yet he never seemed far away. I heard frequent references to the weather as "good or bad" for daddy. All too often "Daddy can't afford it" ended my plans for football boots, a scout uniform, a special comic and so on. One Christmas we, the children, wanted a Christmas Tree like those we saw in other houses. "Daddy can't afford it", ended that. In it's place mother, undefeated, concocted a delightful one with two wooden hoops "like those children have in Spain". Thus inspired, we produced a wealth of decoration for it and throughout the house.

One interesting thing emerges from my cloudy memories of my father from those early days, the name of his smack, Arbor Vita, perhaps because of it's strangeness. I still wonder why it was chosen.

Of my crowded early memories ships and the sea more than hold their own. I can still see clearly that shipyard on the far side of the wide stretch of water linking Oulton Broad to Lowestoft. I went back time and again attracted by the making of a ship.

I can see as clearly Uncle Albert's house. It was one of a few, isolated on the high bank, it's garden ran steeply down to the water's edge. The high tides flooded it's lower part and left behind very varied debris. He, the skilled craftsman, examined it for "bits and pieces which might come in useful". He stored it systematically around the walls and on shelves in his workshop topped by his pigeon loft.

Beyond Uncle Albert's was that ships' graveyard with, very sadly, one or two smacks left to decay. Masts and funnels leaning all over the place, pieces of rigging hanging loosely added a chaotic touch to the sadness. I wondered why they were abandoned.

Some time later at a spot before I got to Uncle's house, a man started a small ship breakers yard, not so melancholy as the graveyard. People came to buy spars, masts and planking for further use.

My Something was still very active on the day that Mr. Todd – "Toddy", our brilliant martinet of a teacher – ordered, "Choose your own poem. Then learn it!" Which did I select? "The Sea"! I can still recite the first verse:

> "The sea! The sea – the open sea!
> Without a mark – Without a bound,
> It runneth the earth's wide regions round".

I remember only three of the many we learned, and of that three "The Inchcape Rock" only I can still quote.

> "No stir in the air
> No stir in the sea – The ship was still as
>   she could be.
> Her sails from heaven received no motion,
> ˌHer keel was steady in the ocean.
> With never a sound or sign of the shock
> Her keel rode over The Inchcape Rock."

I joined the Lowestoft Carnegie Library as soon as I could, for which I paid one penny (old money!). On my first visit I stayed until closing time and sorely tried the patience of the librarian. I turned away book after book until I asked for one called "The Rover", which I then rejected because the hero had nothing to do with the sea. Finally I took "Swiss Family Robinson". It began and ended with – the sea – I read and re–read it and made sketches. I did the same with "Masterman Ready", my ideal of a sailor who could do so much and was so like Grandfather Macey!

It does seem that my Something, thus much exercised and encouraged, must have strengthened my arguments with my parents and won a victory, which, as I stood alone on the quayside, I bitterly regretted.

Chapter 2

Getting Ready – We Go to Sea!

I did not have to make that frightening leap. In the few minutes I stood on the edge of the quay, growing more and more miserable, I noticed that the gap between the ship and myself widened and narrowed as she swung at her moorings. At it's widest I could see more of that greasy green water below.

Then father called, "Come along, Billy". I was so glad when he reached out one hand and swung me easily into the rigging. This was a rope ladder rising steeply from the bulwarks and joining at the top of the mainmast. I found the rungs gave me very little support, they sagged too much. I was relieved again when he lifted me down to the deck. The first thing I noticed, strangely, was it's narrow planks!

"Sit over there", father said, "and don't get in the way". He indicated a wide timber around the stern forming a kind of seat. He went below. A more miserable, self-critical young boy surely never existed! Something in father's manner, and his voice, had increased my misery.

A few minutes later he re-appeared on deck in his sea-clothes – they were any cast-offs that could stand the wear and tear for a trip or two. He ignored me. He turned to the two men. Each clearly waiting for instructions. That slight earlier doubt now crystallised into cold certainty. He was not the father I knew at home. He was different in voice, manner and exuded a masculinity, so different

Waiting for Skipper

from the quiet, almost self-effacing man I knew. The family would not have recognised him.

A few quiet words and the crew set to work, he with them. I was to learn that they were getting ready for Skipper – "He might want to leave for sea straight away". I looked around me. Everything seemed even more mixed up and incomprehensible than when I first saw it from the top of the quay.

It was so much quieter, almost peaceful, after the hectic life of the market. I had expected loud words of command and some "Aye, aye sir", and "Go to it, me 'earties" of fiction – not at all. I cannot recall a single "sir", then, or ever. Father almost asked or at times seemed to suggest that the men should do such and such a thing.

Completely isolated, seemingly abandoned by father, I longed for my familiar world.

Then, suddenly, I heard a great shout from above me. "Crimson Rose! Grocer!!" On the quay stood a rather small man and by his side a large basket. Someone appeared from below, they called him "Cooky". He helped the caller and his basket down to the deck. Together they checked the contents. Both satisfied, the grocer's man departed, Cooky went below with the groceries. He had no sooner disappeared than he was up again, just like a jack-in-the-box, in answer to an equally loud but rather piping voice, "Crimson Rose ! – Baker!!" He stood up there, small, very young, beside his basket from which peeped a loaf or two. Cooky had to help him down with his load. He checked it. He disappeared below. The baker's boy went.

I heard a chugging, growing louder, from behind me. I looked and saw a low in the water launch approaching us quite quickly. It had a tall, cigarette like funnel with wisps of black smoke. Its narrow deck, so narrow that I feared for the safety of it's two man crew, bordered the hold filled to over brimming with glistening, crushed ice. As one man moored her to Crimson Rose, the other shouted, "Crimson Rose!", and began to fill one of the baskets standing on the deck. Up popped Cooky. He lifted a small metal lid fitted into the deck near the companion way. He checked the number of basked loads quickly shot into the hole. He carefully booted in the pieces of ice which had missed. He clanged back the lid. With the customary "So long", the ice wherry chugged away.

By this time Cooky was below, but only for a few minutes. Another stentorian call assaulted my ears, "Crimson Rose!!". This time it was the butcher. He handed over to jack-in-the-box Cooky a number of luscious looking, large cuts of meat. He did not go below immediately. Instead, lifting the lid of the hole through which the ice disappeared, piece by piece he carefully packed the meat into it. He closed the lid. He disappeared, but, again not for long. He was recalled this time by a man holding the metal nozzle of a slender, shiny black hose snaking behind him – into the unknown. He wore heavy boots, a long waterproof apron and the official peaked cap of the Great Eastern Railway. Cooky lifted another lid near to the other but much smaller. The man fitted in his hose. I heard the water gurgling down. How Cooky estimated the number of gallons I don't know. He signalled enough. The man released the nozzle. He left, the shining black hose trailing behind him. Cooky fixed the lid and went below. He had yet another call. A replica of the ice wherry but much, much grimier, also with a two man crew, was quickly tied to Crimson Rose. One man shouted "Coal–l–l!" whilst the other quickly filled a basket and carried it on to our deck. Cooky popped up yet again. He took up another lid from the deck very near the others, and about the same size as the one used for the ice. Just as quickly the men shot in baskets of coal until Cook signalled "Stop!". He carefully swept in pieces of coal and all traces of dust. He replaced the lid. By now the coal wherry was away to it's next customer.

The coal men ended Cooky's performance as jack–in–the–box, but, instead of returning below he joined the others, including father, sitting around smoking and chatting. They had clearly finished, "getting ready for Skipper", and were now, "waiting for Skipper". With the ending of movement and interest my loneliness and doubts returned, intensified.

Another man confidently leapt from the quayside, the mere thought of which had scared me. He clambered down the rigging to the deck. Father met him. They were both the same height and about the same age. He was less bulky than father. His smart shore clothes made father look even more tatty, but none the less he still looked ordinary. Father brought him to me, "Skipper", he said, "this is my second boy, Billy. He wants to come with us".

For some inexplicable reason I wanted him to agree! He said nothing for a moment or two – I saw two keen, penetrating eyes set in a rather pallid, sunken cheeked face. It had a thin lipped mouth, it's sternness emphasised by two marked lines stretching down from either side of his nose. A man to be reckoned with! Finally he said, "That'll be alright".

It seems unbelievable to me now that, in those days, a cosseted boy of nine, still a baby compared with the modern sophisticated youngster, should be allowed to go on such a dangerous venture. What about the owner? Skipper did not consult him. What were their – and father's responsibilities in law and insurance? A custom deeply rooted in tradition ignored all these. This was a kind of recruiting campaign. By introducing a boy at such a tender age to a fisherman's life he might find that he liked it and become a smacksman after leaving school. It didn't work with me!

Soon I heard Skipper, who by now was in his sea clothes, say, "We's better go". No barked orders again. It was almost as if the crew just overheard him. The youngest of the men, they called him Decky, jumped to the quayside. He went to a bollard and lifted off the heavy rope looped over it. He dropped it into the water. It was quickly hauled aboard as the ship's bow moved away from the quay. By that time Decky had dealt with a similar rope trailing from our stern.

Crimson Rose, floating from her moorings, reminded me of a horse just released from it's stable and looking forward to the open field as I had read in "Black Beauty", I felt that she too was anticipating her freedom. As we neared the harbour mouth I saw, beyond, the rather wild looking waves, some foam topped. Already the deck began increasingly to rise and fall. My whole being, especially my stomach, wanted to imitate the rhythm. Yet another to increase my long lists of doubts and misgivings – Sea Sickness!

I had heard much about it, especially it's horrors and so called jokes, usually from those who have never suffered it's degradation. The indignity if I got it! Me! With all that sea in my blood! In front of my father! Fortunately I escaped.

On a later trip a school friend came with us. His father was the third hand. We were both young because we both went to the same infants' school. We had just cleared the harbour mouth, and the smack was beginning to bounce about, when he said, "I feel sea sick". In a few minutes he was. It continued off and on for the remainder of the trip, to him, five dreadful days away. As each passed he became weaker and weaker, his face paler and yellower. For the final three his father carried him up from below and laid him on a blanket in the little boat, with the ship's bucket ready by his side. He could not or did not want to speak. He had large dark eyes which seemed to become larger. I can still see them gazing pleadingly up to me. Why didn't his father ask skipper to return to harbour? Both dared not do so. First, because the boy was on board, as it were, illegally. Skipper dared not because it meant at least two days fishing lost. The owner would not like that! Two days fishing lost was serious also for the crew, particularly, for the share-men, skipper and mate.

This was it! No going back now! To emphasise this it seemed that a great door shut firmly behind me. It cut me off from everything I had hitherto known. It left me face to face with a life as different as possible, and, with my father not a bit like the one I knew.

Already I knew that the world had shrunk to the size of a small fishing smack and to which I must adapt, quickly. I do not claim that such deep thoughts were running clearly through my head. I did know I faced something very, very new, and different. I am rather proud to recall that I did not feel afraid.

By the time I fell asleep that night I had met a number of the differences, some very exciting and all, as was to be expected, strange and new. One at least was embarrassing – very!

This must have come soon after leaving harbour because father was still on deck. I had already noticed that everybody went below unless required for something important. They left the man on watch all alone at the tiller. I knew it was not father's turn because Decky was there. I was not sure if he wanted me to call him father or the usual daddy. I decided against both.

"I want to do number two", I said (this was the family euphemism for the more serious of the natural body functions, "number one" being the other). I do not know what I expected when he said, "Follow me". I followed to the area of the open deck near to the butt of the main–mast. "There it is", he said. He indicated a small, stout, wooden barrel – 'the tub' they called it. It was bound by three iron hoops, one at the bottom, one in the middle and the third – the seat! – at the top. I looked at that sharp edge with some misgiving. "Hold on to this", father said, and pushed into my hand a ropes end dangling from the rigging. "You'll need it". I certainly did. Apart from the embarrassing publicity, with Decky grinning at me from the tiller, Crimson Rose, as if to add further to my difficulties, began pitching and tossing more violently. Father returned. "Here's some paper", he said. He handed me some torn sheets of the 'News of the World'. He came back later. He emptied several buckets of sea water into the tub. He tossed the whole contents overboard.

"Number One", they called "pump ship, but never t' wind'd", for a very obvious reason. The height of the rail presented me such problems that I had to stand on an upturned fish trunk.

The embarrassment of the tub disappeared amazingly soon, probably because everybody did it so naturally!

Soon after leaving harbour there came an awful smell. A noisome sludge oozed slowly towards the scuppers. "That's the bilge", Decky said, as he cleaned the deck with buckets of sea water and a

Crimson Rose - defiant! Me right up forrard

18

vigourous scrubbing with the broom, "Oi just thought Oi'd turn't on." An innocent, straight forward remark? Later, when I began to understand smacksman's humour, it could have been "a troiy'n it on", as he would put it, just to see how a young boy's queasy stomach would deal with it! Perhaps I disappointed him because I accepted it!

During the afternoon I went below. I was able to do so now because the strong sea air had cleared away all but a tiny tinge of that first stench. I went to the freshwater tap to wash my hands. "Hi", shouted Cooky, "y' can't do that – that waters f' cook'n – not f' wash'n. A buck't a sea water'll do f' that"!

So my new life began to unfold – rapidly.

Decky and I soon became friends because his was always a day watch. There are few places more peaceful than the deck of a smack bowling along under a steady breeze with everybody down below except Decky. I could hear clearly his low whistling. I trod carefully as father had ordered.

I quickly discovered what was, for myself, the most interesting place on deck as far up forrard as I could squeeze. It soon became a great favourite. Here I felt the animal life of Crimson Rose more firmly, and the resemblance to Black Beauty more clearly. She gathered herself to meet each great wave so confidently, with her bowsprit pointing defiantly towards the sky as she reached the top, often with a burst of spray. She paused momentarily. Then she slid smoothly into the watery valley below. Her bowsprit now jutted so strongly downwards that, at times, it cut into the slope of the next wave. She dealt with wave after wave so much like a steeplechaser – they have the easier task, their obstacles stand still! As for Crimson Rose, hers raced to meet her rising higher and higher as they came. Very rarely did even the biggest come aboard, then only as spray which stung my cheeks.

Very soon I met the smacksman's inseparable favourite, his tea. "'Ere y' are", urged Cooky. "It's not loike what y' ave at 'ome", and, he added "Y' spewn'll stand up in 't!" He was certainly justified

The Smack's mastery

in his first claim. It had the colour of a mahogany stain – and would probably have served well as such. It's texture did lend some support to his second. They downed several mugs of it each day, boiling hot. On a bitter winter's day it would certainly warm their insides – and their hands and nostrils. I came to accept it – slowly.

This unique brew they prepared in a suitably unique way using a tea pot – cum-kettle called "The Shoe", so appropriately because it was a high sided one in metal with a firmly fitting lid. Into it Cooky put the tea, the sugar, the condensed milk and the water. He then opened the boiler door. Into the intense heat he pushed the shoe and the cleverness of it's shape became apparent. He slammed the door back. The shoe must have boiled quickly. How Cooky gauged the length of time for this 'cooking' I know not, but, with his several other jobs, it could have stretched to a quarter, a half an hour, or more.

Round about seven o'clock on my first night father told me he had to stay on deck all night. "I have to take the night watch", he said. Not long afterwards , "It's time you went to bed", he said. I began to loosen my collar – the customary Eton, stiff kind which could be cleaned with a face flannel. By the time he noticed me again I had begun on my jacket – the conventional Norfolk style with a belt and buttons up to the neck. "No need for that", he said. "You can loosen your boots, or take them off if you like". A funny idea of getting ready for bed! As with my "number two" earlier, I had no idea of what to expect next. I followed him below.

"That's my bunk", he said. He indicated one of the rectangular densely dark openings. "You'll be alright in there".

I clambered to the top of his locker and more or less fell into complete darkness. I sat up abruptly and banged my head against the deck beams. I stretched out and immediately noticed the thinness of his bedding. I heard the crinkling of paper beneath it. Fully stretched out, even my toes touched the end. How did father manage?

I snuggled down to sleep. I was dog tired. Within a few minutes I had to sit up. The mixture of stale air, smells from the "bedding" and father's occupancy – no ventilation. "How does he put up with this?"

I scrambled out, but I had stayed long enough to enjoy an unusual but attractive kind of music. It was composed of the rhythmical gurgling, hissing, and slapping of the sea – I suddenly realised only about two inches or so from my ear as I pressed it against the timbers! These and the widely varied in volume, sound and rhythm of the many ship sounds reminds me now of modern music. I very much prefer that of Crimson Rose. I returned more than once to enjoy her tune.

I slipped down to the locker top, wide enough for an uncomfortable bed. A lively Crimson Rose made that impossible and risky. Only the cabin floor remained. So being very young, and very tired, I curled up and fell asleep at once.

Several hours later I awoke because of movement against me, and loud snoring. I turned. There was Skipper jammed against the leg of the cabin table. Near to him, I saw – and heard – Cooky. Where was Decky? Later father explained, "He's the only one who can stand his bunk all the time". I never slept in a bunk – father did not! I slept once on a locker. The night was very calm.

Heavy noises over my head woke me twice during that night. Both had clumping footsteps but each had a different dominating sound. The first a rasping across the deck, and the other a clanking sound of a heavy chain. With that second one I heard the capstan. With neither did I hear loud commands or voices.

I finally awoke to enjoy the sunlight streaming through the open skylight above my head, dappling the cabin floor with changing patterns as the smack dipped and rose. But it was the aroma which drove even that from my mind. I choose "aroma" as the only word adequately to describe my first experience of Cooky's breakfast fish. "'Ere y' are", he said, and slid a chipped, white enamelled plate across the lino topped cabin table towards me. "Get that inside on y'". I did, rapidly.

I have tasted fish many, many times since and from many different cooks. Not one can fully compare with Cooky's first. It was only round about two hours from the sea! A milkiness oozed from the bone as my fork touched it.

I remember one dinner time – about midday. (The "toff's" midday luncheon and evening dinner was still more than half a century into the future!) We had stew followed by suet pudding with treacle. I poured out a lot too much. Skipper looked at me. It was the first time I faced that expression. I hoped I would never see it again. No wonder he needed few words to run his ship. After what seemed to be a very long time, he said very quietly, "Y' know – y' father 'as t' 'elp t' pay f'r that lot".

Another time, for some reason, Decky was there instead of on deck. Cooky served corn beef, the first I had seen or tasted. "Look at it very carefully", Decky warned, "Look out f'r bits a fur. They make it fr'm cats". This was another very early confrontation with smacksman's humour – nothing subtle, as I already suspected, at times embarrassing and spoken normally with a dead–pan voice and face.

That day, I watched the shooting and hauling of the trawl. The first explained the rasping sound I heard during the night, and the clanking of a chain which aroused me during the early morning – The hauling, they called "th' 'aul'n", and the shooting, "th' shoot'n". I prefer their versions.

Chapter 3

Down Below

Here is a typical example of Suffolk's "if you can get rid of part of a word – do it". So Lowestoft becomes Low–stf, Happisburgh – Hazebro' and "Down below deck" shortened to "down below" and they were even more economical in "Take it below" and "Get below".

I took one step below within a few minutes of leaving harbour on my first trip. Just one step only

had matured. By mid–day I was freely going down below with never a thought of sea–sickness. The ventilation by way of just the companion way and the cabin, both seemingly inadequate, worked quite well at sea.

I copied the men who went down the metal edged steps of the very steep companion ladder backwards. To do otherwise was difficult and dangerous. As I went I noticed the light oak grained match boarding on either side – an unexpected touch, quite expensive, of luxury.

I landed at the bottom in "the engine room" so named because of the little donkey engine attached to a huge round boiler which reached well above

The engine room and Cooky's "galley". Observe: The coal locker, the concrete floor slabs, the one small lamp, the details of the donkey engine, and Cooky's tiny cooking range on which he performed his "miracles".

– just one breath of the air down there. I was so near to sea–sickness! I took one, very hasty jump back. In that short time I detected cooking and damp clothing smells, smells of men, steamy smells mixed with many others indefinable.

In fairness to Crimson Rose, and her skipper and crew, a twenty four stay in harbour with her inadequate ventilation not functioning, that brew

my head. Varnished wooden strips secured by brass rings encased it pleasantly – another unexpected decorative touch. It took up so much space that, with the shelves to the left and an ample box like coal bunker to the right, I agreed with Cooky's comment on the space for his galley "Not enough room t' swing a bloody cat!" His linen line, about head height, festooned with his limpid tea

21

towels and the crew's damp clothing gave him even less room.

By the companion ladder through a pleasantly panelled door I glimpsed the cabin – the small "social" centre into which four or five men could crowd – but never all together. Because one – two in a heavy storm – had to be on deck.

Skipper enjoys a well earned rest in the fug and warmth of the engine room. He is wearing his wellingtons. Observe: the sou'wester and oily frock hanging in the cabin, also "the shoe" and the pleasantly panelled cabin door

On entry the first thing I noticed was the light colouring, pale duck egg blue on the ceiling and the same light oak graining of the woodwork, some of it as pleasantly panelled as the door. It certainly helped to give a feeling of space, but, it made the ceiling look deceptively higher than the mere few inches about my head, especially where the massive deck beams protruded. Many a careless smacksman above average height had painful reasons for learning and remembering this. The overall shape followed the lines of the ship. It tapered slightly forrard where the massive butt of the mizzen mast passed through on it's way down to the keel. On it swung the glistening brass cabin oil lamp. On a broad shelf I saw the beautifully maintained copper port and starboard lights. A row of lockers ranged along both sides, their tops served as seats and – in calm weather – as beds. Above each of these I saw a row of cupboards topped by a wide shelf obviously used by the men for small personal belongings. Above these again the very dark rectangular openings to the bunks caught my eyes. In between the two on the port side hung the all important cabin clock, by which skipper timed the tides. It was second only in importance to the compass swinging above my head in the narrow opening to the skylight, the only source of daylight and ventilation. On the floor the costly "battleship" quality lino appeared, as well kept as the side lights. The one-legged cabin table had strip about an inch or so above it's surface – to keep food and crockery on top in heavy weather! The far end of the table slotted firmly into the shelf which held the side lights. Drawers and cupboards, all grained and panelled, flanked the cabin entrance. On the port side of East Dean's cabin door was a fireplace.

I still have the impression that the owners did try to give the cabin "a way from it all" with these touches.

I contained myself, until the third day of my first trip, before I dared explore the mysteries beneath those two dark openings in the deck near the main mast. I had two very real fears, one of rats, and the other of sea-sickness, although by that time I had become inured to most of the smells. I have an inbuilt aversion to rats. "Rats", said Decky "Woiy! Oive see'm big as cats a'walk'n along our moor'n ropes". Father's story did not help!

"I was putting on my sea boots", he said. "I'd already got one on. As I pushed my foot down into

Mate in the cabin. Observe: his bunk behind him, the panelled woodwork, the locker top beneath his feet (often used as a bed) and the boiler in the engine room with the "donkey" engine attached.

the other I felt a scrabbling on my toes. So I jabbed down hard two or three times. I took the boot off, turned it upside down – and – out fell a darn great rat!"

I had also heard the horrific story of a sailing ship wrecked on the shore at Yarmouth. From it swarmed hordes of rats which scattered the horrified spectators.

For my first venture I chose the larger of the openings, the one just aft of the main mast. I waited until the trawl was up, so that the coils of the warp gave me a quick and easy way down – and a quick escape in an emergency. Some called this "The Rope Room", I became accustomed to it as "The Main Hold"

What I expected I can't remember, but what I did see and felt surprised me. First, the echoing, emphasised by an occasional gurgle or two from the drinking water tank, invisible in one of the several deeply dark areas. Next, it was almost free from smells and so clean. Then the white paint all over the place especially on the two pipe like columns supporting the deck and on the beams above my head, with the silence, reminded me of the Band of Hope chapel in Oulton Broad where I went to Sunday school. A ghostly glimmer from the ice box helped! Two large cupboard like shapes, side by side and painted white, almost filled the stern side. These I learned were the fish pounds, kind of refrigerators. I noticed that, in the place of doors they had short, narrow planks slotted into what would have been a door frame. As I looked into the deepening shadows up forrard I made out short white railings forming compartments. In one I saw an orderly variety of ropes and in another, surprisingly for "The Rope Room", the massive links of the smack's anchor. With no hint or glimpse of a rat, I stayed much longer than I planned. So much for Decky.

I went to the second, smaller dark opening just forrard of the main mast. No coiled ropes to make things easy as I dropped down and landed with quite an unpleasant jarring. The cramped area tapered sharply towards the bows. Some white

Below with "The News of the World"

paint – not much and so, together with the sounds from outside as the waves met the ship, there was no suggestion of a chapel!

I could just see, it was much murkier here, two rows of white posts creating two unequal spaces. In the larger were sails, neatly stored. I learned much later that some were for replacement. Others with special names like spinnaker and storm jib were for special kinds of weather. The smaller area held bales of spare net, coils of rope, and a collection of a smack's odds and ends.

Despite Decky's warning, "That's where y' must expect to meet'm", I neither saw nor heard one.

Chapter 4

Shoot'n and 'Aul'n

"Shoot'n and 'aul'n the trawl" – the smacks I knew existed because of them. When the beam trawl was first fitted they soon realised that the ship of the day had to be modified. Especially it needed a second mast with it's sail at the stern, not at the extreme end but a few feet in from it. Among it's – the mizzen's – advantages, I was told, was that the smack could be left unattended during shooting and hauling so freeing an extra much needed man. The massive beam of the new trawl meant that the ship had to be more than a certain length. One they found too short, so her shipwrights sawed her in two. They fashioned, inserted and fastened in a piece to do the job and away she sailed a-fishing with her brand new beam trawl.

My first shoot'n began late afternoon of my first day out. Skipper came on deck. He looked around. "I reck'n we'll shoot", he said to the man on watch. How he made up his mind I can still only guess! He went to the open cabin skylight and shouted, "Trawlo–o–o!!". Within a few minutes all tumbled on deck, and each man to his place – no further orders. To my surprise Cooky dropped down into the dark opening near the main mast. I soon knew why, because a mighty rope appeared from it's darkness and was hauled across the deck – I found later I could barely span it with both hands. To this, the warp, they secured somewhat thinner ropes, the bridles, which led from the two large, open triangular iron trawl heads, one fitted to each end of a solid and long beam, a kind of rejected telegraph pole I thought. All it seemed was now ready.

I watched from inside the little boat. Skipper had peremptorily ordered me to go there. I wondered why, a little bit upset! I was soon to discover the answer. The warp now firmly secured to the trawl lay across the deck quiet and harmless. The men loosened the ropes which held the trawl beam to the side and with a quiet "Heep–Hoip" (the nearest I can get! – and the nearest to a sea shanty I ever heard on a smack) they hoisted and dropped the beam and a mass of netting into the sea. The mighty splash seemed to startle the warp into hectic and scaring life. I noticed the men stood well back. They knew what was coming! It writhed, it coiled, at times as high as my head. It rasped loudly over the deck boards and over the rail, already scoured by it's previous attacks. The beam and the nets drifted slowly away. One end sank abruptly. The other broke surface as if reluctant to go, it's triangular head resembled a sea monster with it's several feet of beam streaming water forming it's neck and mane.

Regularly a barrel organ with it's patient donkey appeared outside our house. The owner leant heavily on his crutch, an iron hook protruding from his right coat sleeve turned the handle. His repertoire exhausted, he limped slowly from door to door.

"The warp caught him", said Aunt Sarah. It broke his left leg, crushed his left foot, and, so mangled his right arm that they had to replace it with that repellent iron hook.

The warp slowed and then stopped. It now stretched across the deck about my waist high and as rigid as an iron bar. What I had earlier dismissed as a hopeless muddle of ropes and netting had become an efficient machine.

Father looped the loose part of the warp around the tow post, a massive timber, shoulder high to me, near to the companion way. He secured it with a surprisingly thin rope by a knot with a surprising name – "The Nettle".

"Th' warp got me"

Trawl down

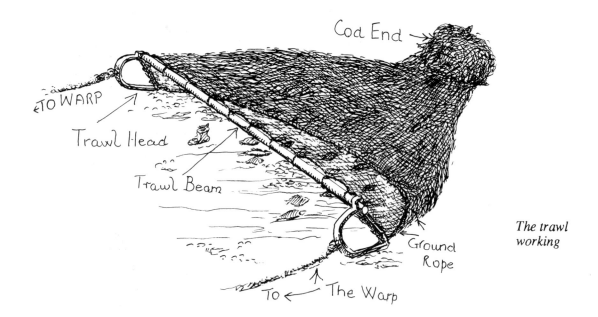

Cod End →

←TO WARP

Trawl Head

Trawl Beam

Ground Rope

TO ← The Warp

The trawl working

Skipper went to the rail, leaned over and firmly grasped the warp with one hand, whatever he learned clearly satisfied him. He spoke to father and went below – how wrong my first impression had been! Decky alone remained on deck.

By now, back on course, Crimson Rose set herself to a task, which would have severely tested a large team of shire horses, hauling against the pressure of the sea and the bumpiness of the sea bed that highly efficient – but very heavy and clumsy fishing contraption.

No sooner had the shoot'n ended when my imagination took over. What was happening down there? I saw the trawl bumping erratically over the sea bed. I saw it's gaping mouth the width of the beam and as deep as the trawl heads. What would be swept into it's gaping jaw and through the net trailing behind it to be trapped in the cod end? Would it be treasure, doubloons and all that? I knew the Spanish Armada had scurried over the sea where we now were. I knew of the great, encrusted anchor trawled up by a Lowestoft smack and authenticated as belonging to one of it's fugitives. Would it be fascinatingly ancient, just like the two mammoths' bones, landed by Grandfather Macey? Father once brought home a lovely piece of amber which had landed on his deck from his cod end. I might find a large packing case, such as came to one crew. Understandably excited, and dreaming of valuable salvage, they opened it. They saw layer upon layer of boots, all new, all shiny and unharmed by sea water – but – they were all for the left foot! Skipper said "There

must be a 'ell 've lot of one legged buggers where this lot wor a goin' to!". I did not want to see any grim finds – bodies or parts of them.

An almost complete skeleton came to one cod end. "Pick'm up", said Skipper to ancient Cooky. He obeyed. The ship lurched. It's arms clutched Cooky's neck, "Go on, Jimmy", urged Skipper "'e luvs y'. Kiss'm!"

A rotting orange rammed into an old boot was my outstanding find.

No sooner was the trawl down than I was looking forward to the 'aul'n.

How did Skipper time it? He reappeared on deck. He spoke with father. I heard him say, "I reck'n, Billy, it's toime we 'auled". I noticed he leaned over the side and grasped the warp, as he did at the shoot'n, before he spoke to father. Did that tell him that fathoms down the cod end was nicely filled? Did his glance at the sky help him to decide one way or the other? Did father influence him?

I had asked him if he thought Skipper would let me call up the men. He must have mentioned it. Skipper looked at me, "Would y' loike t' call'm?" I walked miles tall when they responded as readily to my shrill treble and went as quickly to their places. Two of them went to the side, Skipper to the capstan, father to the tow post, and Cooky into the hold.

Father freed the nettle. Skipper wound the loose coils of the warp around the capstan leaving enough to wind down to Cooky in his semi–darkness. Skipper started the capstan and slowly, very slowly at first, the sodden, dripping warp with an occasional

26

festooning of sea weed came in over the side, across the deck, around the capstan, over the short space and the coping around the opening and down to Cooky. All alone he had to organise it into regular coils ready for the next shoot'n.

I marvelled at the power of the capstan – not as tall as me and only as round as our small table at home.

What blessings the capstan brought to the men – although some had staged a strike against it! Both father and Grandfather Macey spoke of the back breaking labour of their pre–capstan days. I could easily imagine four men against a laden trawl and the tension of the sea, toiling round and round on a deck, made treacherous by the dripping warp, pushing and pushing against the chest high bars of the hand capstan. I could also see them fighting with the great mains'l in a high wind!

At times the capstan faltered, even stopped. Skipper stood on the warp, treated it like a trampoline and on it went mud, sand, sea water, seaweed and all down to poor Cooky.

"It c'd be nasty", he said, "many a toime Oive bin knocked fla', 'n, more'n once thrown on deck". He did not say whether these happened when he was a boy cook.

One trawl head appeared. The sea weed, as well as the water swishing from the exposed length of beam, made it more like a sea monster than ever. As the whole beam came near enough, with another "Heep–Hoip", they leaned far over the side. Then, again supported only by the few square inches of the knees of their leather sea boots against the bulwarks, they man–handled it up to the rail and secured it.

I was able to get close to them. I even offered to help, no danger this time from the warp. I now glimpsed the net streaming away from the ship. They leaned further out now, still only supported by those few square inches, and grasped big handfuls of net, hauled them in and dropped them at their feet. As they stretched over the side an occasional wave surged up to a man's shoulder or splashed his face.

I heard the story of one skipper's young brother who, less experienced, probably enthusiastic, overstretched. A larger rogue wave swept him overboard – but before his brother could do anything about it, the next wave threw him back. Having seen shoot'n and 'aul'n I can believe it.

"'Ere's th' cod end"

The cod end, looking well filled, bobbed slowly towards the side until it was near enough for father to hook the block and tackle from well up the mizzen mast to a loop in the cod end. They wound the rope around the capstan. All was about to be revealed. The capstan clattered into life. The cod end slowly emerged, it looked nicely filled. It rose higher and higher until, with a mighty swish of water, it swung violently across the deck like a great, grotesque, prickly pear. Even as it swung inboard a few tiny captives slipped to the deck and flip–flapped towards the scuppers, as if they knew that was the way of escape. The capstan stopped and in the silence Skipper steadied the cod end.

Only a few inches at the knees for safety

"Wots in 't?"

"Would y' loike t' 'ave a go at th' next bit?" he said. I glanced at Decky's face. There was something there, and in Skipper's voice. "Just pull that little rope", he said. He pointed to a small length dangling from the bottom of the cod end. I pulled – and something said, "jump back". I just missed a sloshy wet mess now above my waist. Was this was my introduction to smacksmens' humour?

Father brought it home when he "played whiskers" – his name for it, but to us a bear like hug during which he rubbed, vigorously, his bristly face against our tender cheeks. He "played" it when he first arrived home with several days growth. Safety razors it seems had not reached the smacks and to shave at sea with a cut throat! Perhaps it was "whiskers" which alerted me, but Decky's face had revealed something.

The catch now more or less conical in shape, looked very big and satisfying to me. "Is this a good one", I said to father. To put such a rhetorical question to a Lowestoft smacksman and to expect a direct answer was a waste of breath. I cannot remember his reply, but, I am sure it was loaded with reservations.

The cod end swishes in-board

Small and medium sized fish slithered free and flip–flapped scupperwards, they too, knew the way to freedom. A few really large ones caused quite a commotion in the pile as they freed themselves. They flip–flapped noisily and clumsily and slowly scupperwards. A couple of dog fish, cunning eyed and snake like, coiled from the pile and slithered across the deck, one towards me, "It'll 'ave a go at y' boot", said Decky, "'n take care of that spoike on th' top 've 'is 'ead – it'll give y' blood poison'n". Fishermen hated them. They went overboard with the other waste. I can remember shovelling them over. Never landed for sale. Just two in the cod end meant gaping holes and the loss of valuable resting time spent in repairing their damage.

A revealing dogfish story began with the arrival of Grandfather Macey with a plateful of fish carried in a tea cloth – an awkward load over the long walk from his home.

"What is it?", mother asked. It was strange to me. It had the vaguest hint of a whiting, but, it's pinkish tinge was puzzling. Beautifully prepared, it sparkled with freshness.

"Eat it first", he replied, mysteriously, "I'll come back tomorrow. I'll tell you then".

We all enjoyed it. Grandfather returned, "Did you all like it?", he asked. We told him we had.

28

"What was it?", mother asked. "Dog fish", he said, calmly. "DOG FISH!!", she exploded. Her temper was akin to a sudden, short thunderstorm on a summer's day. "How could you! You know they are scavengers! They eat dead bodies! You could have poisoned us!". I had not heard her speak to him like this. Poor Grandfather, because he ignored the widely held opinion of dog fish, his joke fell flat.

This all came back, many years later, when I learned that dog fish was regularly displayed in the fishmongers and cooked in the fish and chip shops and sold as coley, huss, and so on, even as rock salmon. What a turn-about for my despised dog fish.

The next stage "th' sort'n" usually began with a mighty kick from Skipper which scattered the pile and revealed the quality of the catch. Without an order they began to build piles of differing fish, soles, slips (small soles), plaice, lemon soles, roker, dabs, cod, whiting, guernet and the several less common fish like haddock, monkfish and the John Dorey. It took a number of trips before I could identify so many.

At that first 'aul'n I learned of some, four in particular:- the cod so different, the dog fish because of Decky and because that one did seem to have my boot in his sight, the roker in particular because of it's unique shape and Decky's warning against picking it up by it's tail, "A scratch", he said, "'n you'd be poisoned", but even more because of it's repulsive ugliness. "It's face is just like a crushed baby's!", I said to father. For an obscure reason which I have yet to learn, the fishmonger's and the fish and chip shop changed it's name from roker to "skate".

Father introduced me to the fourth when he picked up a fish like a whiting but plumper. "Look", he said and pointed to a largish dark mark on each side of it's head, "This is a John Dorey and those are the prints from Jesus' fingers when he fed the five thousand", which said much for his "board school" teachers over twenty years back.

The sort'n left a messy spread to be shovelled over board – bits of sea weed, a small stone or two, a hint of sand and shingle, bits of wood, even a piece of coal and also a few shell fish, one they called a queen. Cooky took up a large crab. Another I recognised as a whelk; father had brought them home.

"Collect'm", Decky said, "when y' get enough Cook'll boil'm f' yew".

I collected 'm. Cooky boiled'm. I enjoyed the young ones. I found the older ones too rubbery.

As I bent down to pick up one whelk, it scurried away. Father said it was empty and "A hermit crab

Cooky finds a crab. Note warp coiled around the tow post, the trawl is down.

now lives in it!". I have learned since that hermit crabs are small, they have no shell and so defenceless, they creep into an empty whelk shell which then becomes it's home and fortress.

"Th' wash'n" followed "th' gutt'n". This seemed to be Decky's job. He stuffed fish into a bag of netting. Attached to it was a length of rope which served to close it and leave enough for him to drop it over the side and vigorously dowse it up and down in the sea racing strongly by. I wanted to help. "Just troiy t' lift it", he said. I failed. "Guess what'd 'app'n if y' dropped it overboard". An action which he performed so effortlessly. "You'd be a goner in no toime!".

All the muck overboard, Decky drenched that part, and scrubbed it thoroughly with the hand deck broom, until it arrived at the state which satisfied Skipper.

By now the catch duly gutted, cleaned and separated by kind into wooden fish trunks, waited near the opening by the foot of the mainmast. Along came Skipper to do the stowing, Father as mate occasionally deputised. He was examining the net for damage by the dogfish and under-water objects. I wanted to help!

"Come along then", he said. He took one hand and swung me down the mountainous pile of the warp, still damp from the sea. I scrambled into that unexpected quietness and an equally surprising resemblance to my Sunday School.

Bloody dog fish!

noises above my head woke me up on my first night at sea. I heard the clumping of heavy feet, the rasping of a thick rope, the short clanking of a heavy chain and the noisy rattling of the capstan – but only the occasional word. I hurried on deck and into a picture which would have inspired Rembrandt.

Two spitting, flickering, brightly burning naphtha lamps, the shape of a small watering can, gave a Macbeth witches' light, which flung lengthening and diminishing shadows across the deck and upon the lower stretches of the mainsail and mizzen. Its weird glare intensified the darkness of the

The fish trunks now on the floor, Skipper removed some short white planks slotted horizontally into a solid wooden framework also painted white. He slowly revealed an ample zinc lined cupboard. Skipper covered it's floor with several shovels full of ice which he took from a storage area away to the left. (So that was where those basket loads finished up!).

He then very carefully arranged the soles and slips upon this layer. He shovelled in more ice until the coverage satisfied him. He turned now to the plaice, these arranged and adequately covered he dealt in the same careful way with the rest of the catch. He then replaced the boards which thus became the door of what was the smack's refrigerator – she had two of them, side by side. They did their job well. Mother never queried the freshness of the fish brought home by father. Some of it, at times, must have come from the first layer, which meant it was at least four to five days from the sea.

Colouring my memories of both shoot'n and 'aul'n is the confident and quiet efficiency with which they turned that seeming muddle into an efficient trawling machine for a ship under sail.

Hauling at night was an unforgettable experience. I remem-ber my first vividly. Several

night to a deep velvety, bluey black, broken only by an occasional twinkle of a phosphorous topped wave, by flickering reflections on the water and on the shiny wetness of the trawl beam. It turned the crew waiting by the port side into brightly lit silhouettes against this intensely dark background. Skipper away to the right appeared and almost disappeared as the flame dipped and flickered and swayed. The lower lengths of the ropes and rigging were lit up, the rest did not exist.

This continuing lightness and darkness, and the constant movement of light and shadow, gave the same mystery and out of this worldliness to everything that followed.

I remember the cod end as it emerged from the sea and swung over the deck more like a huge, grotesque prickly pear than ever. Momentarily the light gave it a sparkling phosphorescent beauty as it flickered over the projecting fish and pieces of debris.

The light moved from man to man as they gutted. It caught an arm, a wet sea boot, a face, a hand, the fish it grasped. It sparkled from the rapidly moving blade of the shet knives. It glistened from the speeding gulls as they wheeled and dived for the flying offal.

Rembrandt would have loved it all and as I "settled down" to resume my sleep on the cabin floor, soon to be rejoined by Skipper and the others, I knew that I had loved every moment of it.

I must return to the gutt'n to introduce the mysteries of the gulls. The men either sat on an upturned wooden fish trunk with a bucket nearby or near enough to the side to make one unnecessary. Each worked with his own multi–purpose, razor edged shet knife. The worked skilfully and swiftly. "No gutt'n f' you", said Skipper when I volunteered. "Too risky". As I watched I had to agree.

The offal, straight into the bucket – and never a miss. Those near the bulwarks, straight into the sea and I am sure – almost! – that as the first gull mouth watering morsel left the blade of a shet knife the first bird came, and, very soon we had a wheeling, diving and raucously screaming crowd. I enjoyed their effortless flight, their graceful wheeling, swooping and diving, and their speed and accuracy to rescue a piece before it sank too far. I deliberately threw some straight into the sea – a sudden splash, an immediate upward sweep and, with never a miss it seemed to me, morsel in beak and a bird swept far into the sky. I did not like their raucous noises, their screaming, their wailing, their quarrelling and their thieving from one another in flight, although very skilful. After the final piece they left us quickly and as mysteriously.

Often one stayed. With a mere flick of the tips of it's wings it swept the length of the ship and back just above the main mast. It's cold, grey, unwavering eyes fixed on me. It mewed quietly. It stayed for some five minutes. Then, suddenly, it departed and left me with yet another query to add to the other gull problems, all by me still unsolved.

First I am convinced the early ones came immediately gutting began. They left when it ended. That one stayed.

Next we were an isolated tiny speck in a wide open stretch of the North Sea. How did they know we were about to begin gutting? Have they an early warning system which enabled them to arrive at the moment we began?. Where did they go, all at the same moment, when gutting ended? Why did they go? Did they receive another pre–gutting message that another smack was about to begin? Why did one stay with us? Was he or she special with a special duty? Why the sudden departure, the job finished, or called away?

Do these mysteries help to explain, in part, the undeniable special relationship between fishermen and gulls?

Gutt'n begins. Then the gulls come! Where from?

Chapter 5

Weather

We had three kinds – mother's, mine and father's. The first two were much alike. They allowed mother to get on with the housework with the rain, wind and snow outside – but, especially on washing day, no rain. To me, not concerned with dripping washing, so long as it did not keep me indoors for too long it did not bother me. To all smacksmen it was all important. To them it was an alliance of "the weather", as understood on land and the North Sea. It helped, it hindered, it tantalised, it threatened. When father wrote, "we had to come back yesterday because of the weather", he was describing heavy seas and storm force winds, an alliance so threatening that even a smacksman gave way.

At times he spoke of icy decks, spray freezing as it struck the rigging, fish turning to ice as it shot from the cod end and as he handled it.. Even then he did not turn for home. The other member of the alliance, the sea, was not playing up.

The sun shining, a calm sea, scarcely any wind. Lovely for us, no good for father. He did not bother about the sun, or whether it was warm or cold or even freezing. With any one of those, or a mixture, but with a good steady wind he could do his job. His good "weather" was The Alliance – the wind, the North Sea, being kind and helpful. The weather of father's letter I call "The Unholy Alliance"..

We lived within sound of the sea. At night as I lay in bed, often with the clothes over my head and plagued with worry for father, I heard the roar and crash of the Unholy Alliance on the beach and against the cliffs. The wind attacked my bedroom which faced the sea. It tore at my walls and frequently brought frightening tremors. It screamed

After just one night!

against my elderly casement windows which rattled and strained as if ready to land on my bed.

Early one morning, after a particularly bad night, I hurried to the beach and saw the power of the Unholy Alliance in a truly bad temper – devastation in a few hours. In that mood man can do little, if anything, even to minimise it's power.

It had grabbed huge lumps of the crumbly, sandy cliffs. Once above them a road ended and houses stood. I saw piles and smears of earth, turf and tarmac widely scattered over the beach, and with them bricks, tiles, shattered window frames and a door. I saw a drain pipe jutting a foot or so below the jagged edge of the road and a gas pipe looping downwards. I saw also bits of furniture. I saw a bedroom obscenely revealed in a shattered house now teetering on the edge.

Father returned two days later. He said nothing about the storm.

Lowestoft Town Council boasted, unwisely, to build the sea wall of all sea walls. Against it the Unholy Alliance would howl in frustration! They even created a concrete road for racing cars and bikes. I saw it quite a time after completion, following another wild period. Perhaps the Unholy Alliance had resented the boasting and so the latest in sea defence thinking, technology and materials paid for it.

I saw deep, irreparable crevices and cracks, lumps of concrete tossed here and there and twisted metal girders. Neither a car nor a bike would ever race there!

During one of it's unholy moods it invaded the town. Round by the bridge, which links the north and south Lowestoft, it flooded stretches where trams, horses, carts and bicycles should have moved. It lapped against the walls of shops and houses and the one around St. John's Church. How it cut me off I never knew. A mass of deepening, swirling water stretched between me and my way home. I managed it, but ruined a newish pair of boots – a tragedy – "I don't know what your father will say", mother said – but he only asked me, "How deep do you think the water was?"

Possibly The Alliance had a quirky sense of humour. It decided to play a trick on Lowestoft's south beach. It chose one night when the moon was high and the tide very full. It began to scour the beach of it's sand. It swept quite a lot of it on to the esplanade, inches deep in places. The rest, a massive amount, it carried out to sea and mischievously dropped it on the spot where it could cause most trouble, at the harbour mouth. Here for years a

Heavy weather

dredger appeared periodically to clear the sand deposited naturally by the sea. Back they came and remained for a long time. Where had been a beach called The Children's Corner, it left some sand, and a wide scattering of rocks and lumps of concrete, some small, others very big. A modern child would welcome it as an exciting adventure playground.

I battled, often excitedly, with the landlubber's bad weather, a mixture of wind, rain, frost and snow. At times the wind became solid and dense enough to lean against. I fought forward, very, very slowly. When laced with sleet and snow it made even shallow breathing painful and my nostrils sore. When a mightier wave crashed and burst against the sea wall, some thirty feet below me, and just as far away, the pavement shuddered and spray splashed my face. No matter the number and thickness of the layers of my clothing the cold cut through to my skin.

If I glimpsed a distant smack battling for home. It could be father. I hurried, as quickly as the wind allowed, to the end of the South Pier where it forms one side of the harbour mouth.

The smack fought nearer. Even if the wave drenched figure standing alone at the tiller was a stranger, I had to stay, mesmerised by the seemingly uneven battle – one small sailing ship and one man against the Unholy Alliance at it's most vindictive. He stood firm as a great wave lifted her bow. I saw gallons of sea cascading from her exposed keel. Another hit her and swept from bow to stern. She shuddered as if to rid herself of the weight of the intruder. Everything rattle–able rattled as she rose and met the next wave, sea water raced from her scuppers. She mastered it – and the next. As she moved into the quiet and safety of the outer harbour, her skipper looked back and waved.

The Alliance had other unpleasant tricks.

More heavy weather!

One – some would consider it's sequel slightly funny – when it tried one on father and made him, by no means a swearing man, blaze forth, even involving the Almighty! It flattered only to deceive by laying on a helpful sea and very helpful wind, ideal for sending the ship moving merrily with her trawl bumping sweetly along the sea bed. He shot and went below to enjoy an always welcome bit a "shut oiye".

Then came the fun, for The Alliance, – the wind died, a dead calm came upon the sea. The trawl was now a useless, hampering collection of netting, timber, metal and rope and a nigh on motionless ship. So up comes the trawl. Skipper and crew return below. Later back comes the "helpful" wind and sea. Up comes skipper and the crew. Down goes the trawl. All again relax below. Later, the wind and sea drop away, once again a useless trawl, a motionless ship, and a very irate crew – especially father.

This continued and finally he snapped. He strode towards the bows, fists clenched. He raised his arms above his head and shouted, "You grey haired old So and So up there. If you want poor fishermen to starve, why not let'm starve at home!"

At times it decided to do nothing, except an occasional useless puff of wind and a slightly bigger wave. It wasn't dangerous, just "roit narsty". My stomach rebelled with even a tiny hint of sea–sickness. Under a peculiarly luminous, dirty grey sky everything on board that could sway, swayed. Everything that could rattle, rattled and squeaks came from everything that could squeak. The glassy sea reflected, mirror like, the unpleasant sky in it's cod liver oil like surface..

Each wave the same height and the same distance apart heaved by with a tryingly monotonous rhythm. At times a tiny puff of wind, with a slightly taller wave, disturbed the ship, and us, and caused the mighty main boom and the massive mizzen boom to crash over with a sound like heavy gun fire, testing to the limit their ropes and blocks. They called this particular trick "a ground swell".

Yet another ploy, not so trying and which might not interfere with the fishing, but "required a bit a' watch'n", came with a brash, bright to hazy sky, slowly covered by heavy inky clouds. An electric atmosphere and the possibility of a thunderstorm, "Tempesty" they named it. One mid–morning at sea it created the most astonishing, and certainly one of the most beautiful weather pictures I have ever seen.

It began with brilliant sunshine from a clear blue sky but accompanied by the usual heaviness and lassitude, which marks the threat of tempesty weather. Slowly heavy clouds gathered ahead, then to port, to starb'd and finally astern. All around us a darker and darker grey, changing to an inky blackness reached to the sea, enclosing us in a space a mile or so across. Yet, above and around us, from an unclouded blue sky the sun still shone as brilliantly upon our small, private world. Lightning flickered and flashed about it's cloud barrier from which came peal after peal of thunder. A cascade of rain almost obliterated it and created a circle of foam as it met the sea. Still the sun shone from a clear sky. Not a drop of rain reached us. The tempest cleared. It never touched us.

The smacksmen never seemed to doubt that their own smack could deal with anything that the Unholy Alliance could hurl at her. Lowestoft was still very much a smack trawling port. Cooky of East Dean clearly showed his opinion of "them new fangled steam trawlers", which were inevitably to replace him and the smacks.

We were on deck on a very breezy day. The waves threatened to come aboard, but never did. We watched a nearby steam trawler. She was making very heavy weather with waves frequently breaking over her bows, and, occasionally over her wheel house. "Look at'er", said Cooky, "She's a waller'n loike a fat arsed ole duck!"

There were times when a skipper was "caught out" and paid the price. A retired smacksman told me this story of two.

"Oi was on deck one morn'n early", he said, – he was probably the mate, "when skipper came on deck. Call 'em up", he said. "We've got t' short'n sail". Very surprised they obeyed. "What 's got into the ole man? – Th' weather wuz so good".

He wondered still more as a nearby smack continued with full sails. "D'you know", he said "Within a few minutes there wuz a 'owl'n gale. We wus alroit" – The other ship was in a "shock'n mess. It's crew must 'ave wondered what our skipper 'ad got an' their's 'adn't"

Skipper caught out! A rare event

At home father was more reliable than the recently introduced broadcast weather forecast. I heard that some skippers preferred the police and sporting programmes than "t' listen'n t' them there blokes – what do they know about our weather?"

Hoping to shop, go for a walk or play tennis and especially on washing day, we continued to ask his advice. He reacted in the true Suffolk manner by inference rather than directly. So he usually began.

"If I were you ...", or, "I don't think ...", or, "It would be a good idea ..." "If you do go, it'll be best if you take your winter coat" or "I wouldn't take a dog out in this". He found "it" still worked when after retirement he and mother lived with me on the outskirts of Epping Forest, many miles from the sea.

Just like old times he came down, hair tousled, still in his shirt sleeves and stockinged feet and stepped out of the back door – "the companion way" – and on to the garden path –"the deck!" He took the customary number of steps – He studied the sky and the trees, pondered at length and then made his pronouncement. Just like the old times.

All went well for a long time. Then I noticed he took longer and longer to make up his mind. He gave his verdict less confidently. "I can't make up my mind these days", he said. "Do you know", he continued, "I reckon it's them scientists mucking about up there". Today there seems to be quite a hint of the truth in his grumble all those years ago.

Whenever I think of my smacksmen and weather, the picture of the instrument panel considered essential for the safe conducting of today's trawler comes into my mind. It's complexity, and multiplicity of knobs, switches and dials reminds me of the one on a jumbo sized passenger plane. When I saw it on a Lowestoft modern trawler I suddenly realised that a smack's skipper had those switches and knobs in his head. He used each one on demand. "Oi don't go wi' them new fangled contraptions", he would state, probably indignantly, "Oi don't feel th' need on 'm". One switch which he would strenuously oppose, the ship to shore telephone. "Oi don't want them on shore allus a barg'n in, 'n tell'n me what t' do".

Chapter 6

Homing

I am using "Homing" for this account of my return to Lowestoft from my first trip which had lasted more than five days. The length of each one depended upon several factors, two in particular, the size of the catch, and bad weather. Skipper decided when to come home with no possible means of discussing with the owner. This and all my returns left me with a puzzle, as baffling as that

I knew we had sailed far, because, the night before I saw a faint glow from the Dutch coast just above the horizon. We had sailed for several hours since then.

Skipper Larko Lark came on deck still in his stockinged feet. He stood for a moment. He walked to the open cabin sky light and briefly studied the compass which rocked there. He turned to Decky on watch at the tiller, "Oi reck'n we'll go 'ome", he said, "Set 'er nor east b' nor". He went below.

Decky leaned on the tiller. East Dean answered. Her sails flapped. Her main boom crashed over. Decky ducked to miss the swinging mizzen boom.

"Set 'er nor east b' nor"

of Uncle Albert's pigeons from far away places. How did they and Skipper do it?

We were far away from home. We had not seen land since leaving Lowestoft. We had sailed here and there for several days, apparently haphazardly. Skipper shot and hauled, and moved on to other places on the sea bed where he seemed to know there were fish.

Uncle Albert, the pigeon racer, with whom I discussed this, said, "Well, there can't be any guesswork about it, otherwise they'd never catch much fish, or find their way home".

Her sails filled and tightened. She swept forward for home.

I looked around at the sea – absolutely deserted, reminding me of a poem I was learning at school – called "The Sea". "Without a mark, Without a bound. It runneth the earth's wide regions round".

How could Skipper know where we were to set such a precise course? I knew Decky could not answer. Neither, later on, could father. He only said, "I expect he knows".

I asked him, "Where are we making for?". "Yarmouth Roads", he said. "What time do you

The High Light

reckon we'll get there". "Oh, round about ten o'clock t'night".

I soon noticed a marked feeling of relaxation. It even seemed to affect East Dean! "They're all a catch'n up with their shut oiy", Decky said of the others. They appeared occasionally and, hastened to the side, "t' pump ship". Poor Cooky had to wait until East Dean docked to catch up on his "shut oiy". The others still wanted their mugs of tea and their grub. Father warned me to move about quietly and not to go below unnecessarily.

One thing only could disturb them, a change for the worse in the weather. No "shoot'n", and "aul'n" and "gutt'n" and net repairing to worry them – until the next trip.

Peaceful hour after peaceful hour floated by. I chatted to Decky and third hand when each was at the tiller. When boredom threatened I went to my favourite spot, well up into the bows. I still believe that East Dean dealt with each wave happily!

Father came on deck to begin his night watch. I asked him how I would know when we were approaching Lowestoft. "Look for a bright light, quite high up", he said. "It'll keep swinging from side to side. Then it'll disappear. It'll quickly come back and go over it all again. It'll keep on doing that. Soon afterwards look for a smaller light low down. It keeps still all the time. When", he continued, "that smaller light is dead underneath the other one, we'll know it'll be safe to turn for the gap in "The Roads". This was probably the longest speech he ever made to me!

I learned later that on either side of that safe gap the water dropped to a dangerous few feet. People had landed there, picnicked and even played cricket.

I stared ahead for the lights too long and too intently. My eyes watered badly. Father sent me below to see the time – just after half past nine! Not too long before his predicted ten o'clock. I returned on deck, waited and stared with growing excitement – we were nearing home and all that promised.

"Look", father said. He pointed. Vaguely in the distance was a light high up. It regularly swept round and vanished. Then I picked out the lower one. At the same time I noticed the lights of Lowestoft sea front. Father judged that the two lights were in a vertical line and turned East Dean to port. We were now heading straight for the shore! Very soon we turned to port again. We sailed parallel to the shore. At times I glimpsed the foam of a bigger wave as it broke on the beach. Skipper now took over the tiller – it was his official task to take his smack into and out of harbour.

I went down to check the cabin clock – about seven or eight minutes to half past ten. Considering

our mileage, father was on target with both time and place. Bearing in mind that East Dean was under sail, and so, at the mercy of the wind, the tide and the currents my question "How did they do it?" grows more puzzling.

As I entered to check the cabin clock Cooky shouted, "Be quick! ... 'n don't come back in a 'urry". It was the same scaring voice, when, at the beginning of the trip, he caught me washing my hands in the water which "wuz f' drink'n 'n not f' wash'n". Later father explained "He's like that as we get near to harbour. Skipper expects him to make everything down below spick and span. You never know who might come aboard to–morrow". When I went below later everything and everywhere possible, especially the cabin, was indeed "spick and span". Cooky was now his usual genial self. Did he boast of his housewifery at home? Very unwise to do so!

Skipper now faced the testing approach to the harbour mouth with it's opposing currents and tide. He must judge when to sweep seawards to round a large bell buoy, followed by an equally delicately judged straight run to the narrow harbour mouth. A small error meant crashing head on to the heavily timbered north pier or on to the sands bordering the south pier.

Skipper, casually it seemed, did all the right things so we sailed through the gap between the two pier heads. It still looked on the narrow side as we swept by with the two pagoda like erections looming, high and black, well above my head.

I have learned from deeply experienced seamen that the approach to Lowestoft is made even more difficult, because, as the charts warned, the depths of the sea and of the sand banks are always changing. It seems that the skippers were wise to prefer experience and intuition.

As we did so I had the same feeling which came when we left – of a great door shutting behind me and cutting off all sights and sounds on the other side.

East Dean moved silently and smoothly towards the docks. Again, as when we left, she became to me a horse but now tired of her unending fight with the sea and the wind eager for her stable.

An intense peacefulness had replaced the noise and unending activity of the market we had left now almost six days ago. The tiniest of sounds were so loud. The slight wavering reflections of the few harbour lights intensified the stillness. It was all rather scaring, increased by the masts of the moored smacks, black silhouettes pointing like fingers into the star lit sky. The bulky dark mass of the market buildings, the intense blackness of it's interior – and the utter silence helped! I am sure even East Dean jumped at the mighty voice, "Oo are yer?" Skipper replied with our name and number. "There's plenty a room in the trawl dock", it said. In the renewed silence East Dean moved smoothly into an ample space between two slumbering companions.

Decky, bow mooring rope in hand, leapt on to the narrow quayside. He looped it over a bollard.

meant up, at the latest, by half past seven to–morrow morning.

Everything now as spick and span and as prepared for the next morning as possible, the crew hurried below. They returned, one by one, each in his shore clothes – and each, like Skipper, a stranger. They muttered sheepishly, "So long", and went, leaving me quite sad. Father went below. He reappeared in his shore clothes. "Come, Billy–boy",

Home!

Third hand threw him the stern rope. This he dropped over another bollard about the ships length away. Safely secured East Dean quickly settled to her well earned rest – for to–morrow could be an ordinary working day. She might well be away again within twelve hours.

Skipper, after a few words with father, went below. He returned soon in his shore clothes, the stranger I met at the beginning of the trip. He said, "So long" (Smacksmen never used "Good–bye"). He jumped ashore and walked away. He had brought us and his ship home. How did he do it?

Father, as second in command, stayed to see that East Dean was left as orderly as possible, ready for to–morrow's market and a visit from the owner. He had to bear in mind that Skipper wanted to catch the early market and be away before midday. This

he said, "Let's go home to mother". He was now the man we all knew at home!

He swung me to the top of the higher quay. I stepped forward, and, but for his quick grasp of my shoulders, would have fallen flat on my face! For quite a distance he had to grip my arm. I wanted the ground to move up and down, the timbers supporting the market roof, and later, lamp posts and houses to sway. A few days at sea had so affected my sense of balance. No wonder, that, smacksmen on land walked, as mother put it, with "a fisherman's roll". Mine eased during the long walk home.

Mother looked at me with horror. "What have you been doing with him! Off to bed with you. I'll clean you up in the morning." The bed felt too soft and warm. I still wanted it to sway a bit. By the morning even that had gone.

Chapter 7

The Smack

I was a small boy when I saw, on the far bank of the water linking Lowestoft to Oulton Broad, the birth of a ship. I must have gone back several times.

I saw first the skeleton. I watched it covered plank by plank – and there was a ship. I remember the launching. I wondered what a horse was doing just walking round and round until the ship reached the water.

wagon and the windmill, in the hands of craftsmen to meet the requirements of the men who used them. So all three have that special kind of beauty which comes from being perfectly suited to their work. I think of a smack in full sail and of a windmill whirling around each so good at it's job. I also think of a teapot, a spoon, a yacht. They all, and many others, have that special beauty which comes from being good to use, good at their work, and therefore good to look at.

If I had seen the birth, and later sketched, a Welsh, an Irish or other fishing boats, I would have noticed differences in each. Some subtle, some clearly to be seen, but, all due to the conditions in

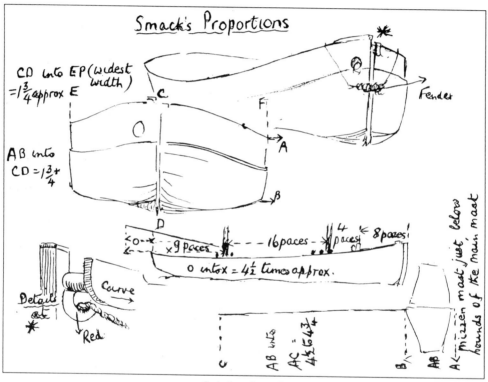

Subtlety in oak

I learned later that the shipwrights I saw had no carefully drawn out plans and possibly not even a half model of a ship to help them. It was not until I began to draw smacks that I appreciated the subtlety of the curves which those men had built, by eye only, into the hull. With that delicate curvature downwards from bow to stern my pencil only succeeded after much use of the rubber. Those men created them in tough oak by eye alone – no rubber!

Nobody sat down, as that man I saw on television, to design a fishing smack. She grew, like the farm

which they had to work and to the requirements of the men who used them. I can well imagine the comments of my smacksman friends if they could have seen that neatly dressed, white coated, television man.

They rarely spoke of their smacks and were almost tongue tied when asked. So I had to deduce a lot.

So to me "Th' ole gal" inferred affection. "Not too bad", guarded acceptance – but "Th bitch!", or stronger, explained itself. I once heard almost enthusiastic, but still inferred, praise from a

Efficiency and grace

Trawl Down

A two reefer or a Three?

unattended throughout shooting and hauling. "Something terrible could happen?" "No", he said. She wouldn't do something terrible if left free for as long as twenty minutes.

An experienced deep sea pilot told me this story. He was taking a very large steamer from the Thames to the Humber. He met a heavy storm off Lowestoft. "I looked down from the bridge", he said, "and saw one of your smacks. She looked like a toy kiddies play with in the bath. She was being swept by waves which, at times, were so big that they made even our ship halt and the spray splashed the windows of my bridge. There was nobody on deck. I'm sure her skipper down in his cabin felt more comfortable about things than I did".

Did the craftsmen unwittingly build a personality into each one? I heard of three built in the same yard. Each with the same choice of materials. All three the work of the same shipwrights. "One wuz alroit". "One took a bit a 'andl'n". The third was such a rogue and caused so much trouble and so many injuries that her owner had almost, "t' broibe men t' sail in 'er".

Harking back to my first trip and the moment when Decky freed Crimson Rose from both her moorings, I felt she came to life, not, as a human being, but as a lively horse freed from her stall and eager to face her usual competitors. Her treatment of the foam topped waves just outside the harbour mouth strengthened my feeling. She reminds me today of a show jumper, but, with a problem which it does not have to solve, her obstacles became taller as they advanced, and, no sooner had she cleared the one, than the next was upon her. Between the two lay a deep and moving alley.

As the days passed I realised how readily she obeyed the tiller and worked with Skipper to deal with all kinds of weather and the trawl. She behaved well all by herself whilst he shot and hauled. She, I feel, joined everybody on board in their dislike of a ground swell which tested Skipper's and everybody's nerves and every inch of her timber, her rigging and her sails.

Above all she proved how ridiculous were my first impressions as I stood on the quay and looked down at her for the first time.

The crew reacted to her as if she were human. Father said of all those he sailed he preferred Crimson Rose. Why, he couldn't say. "There's

smacksman rather overcome by the first sight of his smack fresh from re–painting. "Coo!", he said, quite quietly, "Ain't she a soit f' sore oiyes".

I am certain that to the smacksmen, a smack was as human as themselves. They knew her whims, her behaviour, and they knew how to deal with them and her tantrums. They trusted her. She must be looked after, father told me "Then she'll never let you down.. If she does, nine times out of ten, it'll be you own fault". When I asked him what he did when caught in a really bad storm. "I'd set her properly, batten everything down and lash the tiller. Then I'd go below and smoke, read, or go to sleep. At times I'd pop my head up to see everything was alright".

I sensed the same trust in Skipper Martin's reply to my worrying after I noticed that the tiller was something about her", he decided. She was my favourite too. I do not clearly know why. She was companionable, very co–operative, but not docile. I remember Skipper's annoyance when she would not readily make progress against the wind by a series of manoeuvres carefully timed and carried out. She finally agreed to do so, but only after two or three half–hearted attempts.

I heard a lovely story about Skipper Larko Lark when faced with similar stubbornness from East Dean. She refused to respond fully to her tiller. Once – twice – and with the third failure he exploded. He ran forward. He picked up the heavy deck broom on the way. He leaned over the side. He gave her several tremendous thwacks with the broom, shouting, "Yew stubborn ole bitch! P'raps this'll getcher a goin". She did.

Dainty little Crecy was my second favourite. She was perky and dainty in appearance and action. I often wished I had enough money to buy and convert her into a yacht. With father in charge she would have taken us safely and happily around the world.

East Dean, said to be the largest Lowestoft smack also had "something about her". "She's not easy", was father's opinion. I felt she certainly needed her five man crew. Because of her size she seemed to me stolid and rather unexciting. She had a Skipper's cabin. Larko used it as a dump. Like Crimson Rose she also reminded me of a horse, not an elegant steeplechaser, but a heavy hunter or, perhaps, a Suffolk Punch.

"What a mess", I had thought when I looked down at Crimson Rose for the first time. Ropes all over the place. Nets hanging over the side and covering part of the deck.

Before my first day ended that chaotic mess turned into a workable machine for fishing. I also began to understand that each rope had it's own name, it's own job and it's own very special place for making fast. I very soon noticed also that the men moved safely and easily about the deck which I had thought too cramped and dangerous.

When I saw Crimson Rose, sparkling and resplendent from her re–painting she certainly was in the words of Cooky "A soit f' sore oiyes!" The owners it seemed almost loved to have their smacks "painted up", and more expensively than need be. Gold leaf at "arf a crown a sheet", expensive light oak graining, delicate colours costing more than the more practical black.

It has been suggested that from many years back, the owners had the same feelings towards their ships as gypsies to their caravans – which they still decorate. It is an historical fact that some naval captains, in the eighteenth century, spent more money to decorate the ship than to make her truly sea–worthy.

This feeling must have been still strong for the tight–fisted owners even to think of spending a penny more than was necessary.

There appeared a strong hint of the naval captain in the small delicate leaf carving, together with her name, cut into the bow a foot or so below the rail on both sides of the hull. From there to the stern stretched a narrow groove, also cut into the hull and also gleaming with gold leaf.

Some owners paid a good deal extra for it on the tops of both masts and a lot more for a gleaming weather vane atop the main. Probably, the same men gave more for the copal rather than the usual cheaper varnish for both masts.

I saw the gold leaf applied on a cold and very gusty day. He sat on a constantly swaying bo'sons chair slung by two ropes to the smack's rail. I admired his fortitude. I was fascinated by his skill, the more when the wind tore at the tiny tissue paper like leaves. He pressed each firmly into the cuts – Not one flew away.

They must have used gallons of serviceable dullish black paint for the rest of the hull except the large, beautifully designed initials, LT for Lowestoft, in Roman style, and the registration numbers, 759 for Crimson Rose, in brilliant white which stood out against the black. Below it, just above the water at the stern and the bow, peeped the red, anti–fouling paint which covered all of the hull below the surface.

The more costly, delicate pale green paint they put on the inside of the bulwarks and – of all colours – white on to the rail. The delicate, very skilled graining on the cabin top, the companion way, and, even on the harshly used tow post, must "a cost a pretty penny".

Pale pink on the deck! It came, so they told me, from the water proofing material pressed firmly between the planks. Touches of bright, just as unpractical and more expensive colour, stood out here and there. Red, or yellow, or green, or orange or blue appeared, singly or with one or the other, on the little boat. Here some of the painters seemed "t'ave a go". For fun? For contrast? "No they 'ad a spare tin or so", some said.

From the lovely deep, reddish brown of her recently barked mains'l the same white letters and figures as on her hull stood out.

Crimson Rose was indeed "a soit f'sore oiyes" – but – the life of the delicate colours, placed frequently where they could be scuffed and scratched before the smack left harbour, was very

Crecy in for repairs, father up the ladder!

brief. The owners knew this. Why did they pay the extra?

I noticed during the recession of the nineteen twenties that yellow paint replaced the gold leaf on some smacks.

I am also intrigued by their choice of names – a serious business, as I discovered when I burst into a deep discussion between father and mother and Skipper Frank Martin and his wife. They were debating names, as I thought, for a baby soon to be born. This rather puzzled me. I decided mother and Skipper's wife were much too old! Because of my butting in the debate ended. I was told later that the name was for Skipper's new smack. The one chosen, Crecy, puzzled me. Why Crecy – not one of that four was a historian. There must have been a strong reason. What could it possibly be?

I am still puzzled by the choice of many of the names.

I cannot recall one poetic owner – yet several were attractive and highly imaginative. Here are a few – Blue Haze, Ocean Crest, Rose of Devon, Lily of Devon, Crimson Rose, Golden Buttercup, Glory, Early Blossom.

Sentimental owners were very, very rare! Do these suggest the contrary? Two Brothers, Our Boys, The Boy Jack, Pet, Little Tom, Helping Hand, Susie, Girl Edna, Ruth.

Perhaps with the poetic and sentimental the ladies "took a 'and"?

Literary owners were even rarer, but, whence came George Borrow, Ivanhoe and Pandora?

The following names were to be expected, Success, Pilot Jack, Commander and Master Hand.

"How on earth?" still comes into my mind even as I write the next list – Arbor Vita, The Boy Ramah, Qi Vive, Circa, Telesia, Birca, Crecy, Meum et Trium ('Mum and Tum' on the market!). The last, I discovered, was chosen by Edward Fitzgerald of Omar Khyam fame.

The smacksmen referred to their ships as she and her, never the or it. At times bitch, cow and stronger burst out. The constant use of the feminine pronoun led to anomalies – "Where's the Boy Jack?" – "She 'asn't come in yet" – "Where's th' Commander?" "She's a stern a Ruth".

I rarely heard the word smack. Instead they used "Skipper come aboard very late". "We've got the ice aboard". "Is skipper on board?"

I played on the piles of great tree trunks on the large field, opposite Richard's shipbuilding yard, without realising that they one day would become the hulls of smacks! So I knew them even before the shipwrights! We used the gaps between the trunks as hideouts, pirates' lairs, prisons. The taller

mounds became mountains. Some which jutted out high up teased us into deeds of daring. "Doin' y' dardy", we called it, as the test for admission to a gang. At times a favourite trunk went – for a house, but never, we thought, for a smack.

For a long time I thought all ships were built of oak – perhaps, because we sang loudly and lustily, "Hearts of oak are our ships, Jolly Tars are our men". So I was very surprised when I learned that there were at least sixteen kinds of timber in a smack.

I can see the shipwrights assessing the qualities and deciding the uses of each, which reminds me of a veteran gardening friend with a handful of soil. He studied it closely as it dribbled between his fingers. "It's got 'eart, boy", he said, "It's got 'eart".

Oak remained supreme. First class it went into the hull, and the tow post, which needed it to withstand the enormous tug of the trawl.

Elm, called "the lover of water", they used for parts subjected to constant dampness, her bottom, her keel and her bilge.

They employed for it's strength and flexibility, the Oregon pine for masts, booms and spars. The tree for her mainmast soaring some fifty feet above deck must have been a magnificent sight.

They turned to ash, beech, deal, poplar and scotch fir mostly for down below, all proved by experience as being best for it's job.

Their choice of apple was the most unexpected, as seen in the corners of the triangular shaped sails – the fores'l, the jib and so on – constantly subjected to the rub and rasp of ropes. Apple wood has a tough grain especially when finely smoothed. So, ever on the look out for the "best f' th' job", the craftsmen made from it small, long lasting, smooth eye–lets which the sail makers secured to those particular sails.

How well the shipwrights chose her timbers and how well they built her were proved over and over again. Grandfather Macey's Bella, shattered as she was, with a little first aid quickly and amateurishly applied with bits and pieces left by the great wave, was able to hobble home to Lowestoft. After attention by shipwrights she returned to her trawling, still as tough as ever.

Another smack was caught by a rogue storm off Southwold. It drove her helplessly towards the sandy shore. It humped her on to a sand bank. It tore at her as she stuck fast. With an increase in force it swept her free – but still shorewards – and on to another sand bank. She lay fast, attacked fiercely and constantly by the wind and the waves. Later the storm freed her yet again, only to strand her on another sandy ridge nearer still to the shore. There she stuck, remorsely battered by the storm. The crew took to the rigging until rescued by the Lowestoft life boat. The next morning her skipper and crew stood on Southwold beach. They knew they must do something for their smack to save her from becoming a total wreck – but what?

Skipper had a bright idea. First, the weather had abated enough for himself, the crew, and some very willing bystanders, to get on board. They beached everything possible. This lightened her considerably. Then he roped to her hulk a number of empty barrels. Where he got them from I know not! Southwold has a well known brewery. With their buoyancy, and her considerably re-duced weight, she floated free on the next high tide. The ship-wrights worked as successfully on her as with Bella. So, like her, she resumed trawling. Tough men did deserve such tough ships.

I was never deeply interested in the smack's sails, al-though they attracted me, until I met a retired barker.

I was not allowed to

Summer sails (above) and winter sails (below) by Skipper Osborne (over 80)

have much to do with them. The awful chaos that I could cause by freeing a wrong rope – say, the top sail sheet which could drag me half way up the main mast. I dread to think what would have happened had I meddled with the strangely named nettle, the knot helping to secure the warp which held the complete trawl to the smack. Skipper did allow me to deal with the foresail, in a light wind, it hauled and lowered almost by itself. The way in which Skipper "read" the wind and the sails always remained a mystery.

With perfectly set sails, extracting every ounce of power from the wind she was a lovely picture of efficiency with grace. "Oive know 'm t' go more

th'n twelve knots" they told me, "Y' should've seen 'm move in th' regatter". This was referring to the Lowestoft Annual Smacks event for which owners, skippers and crew did everything possible to beat increase the speed.

Grandfather Macey's painting of it, unfortunately, I have lost.

I needed only a few trips for me to learn the names and some details of the most frequently employed sails – the mizzen, near the stern, the smaller of the two main sails. I learned to duck my head when we changed course and the mizzen boom crash-ed over me head height! The mighty mains'l with it's three layers of reefing points which enabled Skipper to shorten sail, also crashed over, but above the head of the average smacksman. The tall ones had to take care!

I learned that they had a winter and a summer set of sails. For winter they bent the newer, tougher canvas and for summer lighter, older and often patched sails. At the be-ginning of the better weather they lowered the main top mast and replaced it with a taller one which took a larger main tops'l. The smacksmen carried out these changes.

In the meantime I had learned to use the more nautical mains'l and tops'l, instead of the lands–man's main–sail and top–sail!

Intrigued by the man saying he was a barker I looked the word up in the dictionary. It is at least seven hundred years ago when, to prepare skins for leather, a barker barked them in a barking pit.

He gave me the ingredients for the mixture – which he called the cutch – it sounded like a brew for the witches in Macbeth. Shredded oak bark, Stockholm tar, tallow, and red or yellow ochre.

These they mixed, in very hot to boiling water, until it arrived at the condition which experience decided was right for the next stage. They had already stretched and firmly fixed the sail on to the ground. Then they "Sloshed buckets a th' stuff" all over it until it was thoroughly soaked. They rubbed it well in with mops which they made from sacking. They hung it up to dry for some three weeks. As, with all the other stages, experience decided when it was dry enough to be rolled up and delivered to

I learned that because of the cost the owner expected them to last at least five years. When they were "past their best" they replaced the better ones throughout the summer. Some, very pale and even patched, certainly looked their age.

I watched the sail maker in his loft, as, with a bent needle and a glove, he turned some two hundred and fifty square yards of tough, rough and heavy sail cloth into a mains'l, for "ninety odd quid".

Being degraded into a motor smack

the smack. Make a mistake here, he explained, roll it up too soon, "it'd burst inta flames".

It was now the crew's job to bend – not fit – the new sails – a filthy job. I helped – once! It left my hands, my wrists and – unfortunately my clothes splattered with cutch. Mother objected, strongly. When father came home, after a sail bending job, it was in his hair, his eyebrows, even his ears. It smeared his arms and face. It reached his body leaving it's mark on the underclothing.

Barking gave the sails their colour, a rich, deep reddy tan for Lowestoft. Ramsgate barkers must have used more yellow ochre because their sails had an orangey tinge. It gave a sheen, and a texture, resembling smooth thin sheet metal, which was quite a problem when Skipper insisted upon a very neatly furled mains'l.

I heard of a simpler, cheaper cutch. Just red ochre and grease mixed with sea water. This was probably the one used for the annual touch up, which, with an effective first cutch treatment, gave the costly mains'l and mizzen a five year life.

For the smaller triangular jib, fores'l, tops'l and so on, he used a lighter canvas – "that cost'm twenty quid" – expensive when compared with the "ninety quid" for a mains'l (a quid was a pound).

As with most craftsmen there were arguments. These raged over the seams in the mizzen and the mainsails. "Oi reck'n th' verticals are best", "No! Oi reck'n th' horizont'ls are best" ran the argument. I believe the verticals won and for a seemingly negative reason. If filled by an enormous wave it split more quickly, allowing the water to run away sooner and so lessening the danger of capsizing, which was "more loikely t' app'n w' th' other".

A year or two before the second world war, I saw a motor–smack, what a contradictory name!

I knew my smacks had to go. I knew they had enjoyed a longer innings at Lowestoft, by more than twenty years, than at any other fishing port. I resented the manner of their going. Lowestoft destroyed them in a moment of panic, it seems to me, brought by the threat of the second world war. Some they sold to foreigners.

Chapter 8

The Crew

Those we called "big smacks" had a five man crew – skipper, mate, third hand, deckhand and cook. The smaller smacks – the toshers, another fascinating smacksman's word – dispensed with the third hand.

You soon knew who was skipper! Not by any badge of rank. Like the others he usually wore whatever would stand up to the work. Not by his voice, none of that fictional barking of, "Heave Ho! Me 'earties!" (Few smacksmen ever pronounced the letter H). Not by his orders or his manner of giving them, some sounded more like suggestions or hints, often introduced by "Oi reck'n", "It's about toime". The crew, as I noticed at the outset, seemed to anticipate or didn't need them. I was almost able to count the number of orders throughout the entire trip. I never heard a "Sir"! usually "Skipper". I cannot remember hearing "Skip". He and mate generally exchanged Christian names.

A "Tosher" crew. Left to right: Skipper, Decky, Cooky, Mate

I remember the story of a skipper who was "more th'n a bit on th' tough soide". "Why do you stay with him?", I asked. "Well y' see, 'e wor a good seam'n". So all was forgiven. He knew his job. "E wouldn't stan' no nonsense". He must have that something which, although I was only nine years of age, I felt when I met Skipper Frank Martin.

been very much built upon them. It is difficult to decide which held the other in greater respect – skipper or the owner – although the second held the trump card, dismissal.

There was that moment when the owner played a false card at the height of a storm which, for two days, had kept the smacks in harbour. This was the morning of the third day. Skipper was there, the

Skipper: "O' ive got all them knobs in me 'ead". The trawl is down and the "nettle" is securing the warp. Note how the main boom can swing freely, also the cluttered little boat.

I do not remember what I expected perhaps somebody from "Treasure Island"? Perhaps a distinctive uniform? He was not what I imagined, but, only for a moment or two. It was his voice which finally made me feel "there's a man to watch".

Skipper Larko Larke, of the rubicund face, twinkling eyes and humorous mouth, had the same something which made me decide, here is another man to watch.

A bad skipper could not last more than a trip or two, his owner, and his crew would soon see to that. No matter how efficient the business organisation, the smack, it's crew and equipment everything depended upon skipper. The stability and prosperity of Lowestoft as a fishing port, had

crew were there, the smack was ready. The slightest easing of the storm and they would have gone. Once beyond the harbour mouth, short of the change to a hurricane, they would have battled it out. On the quayside were a few onlookers, among them the owner and skipper's young son.

Suddenly the owner, with what he wrongly supposed was smacksman's humour which he thought skipper would take, "Skipper", he chaffed, "I reckon you're feel'n a bit scared!" "Loike 'ell y' do", skipper shouted. To the dismay of the onlookers he jumped aboard. "We'll go", he ordered. "Don't be such a bloody fool", yelled the now frightened owner. He ordered skipper not to go. He took no notice. With his small son standing in the frightened crowd skipper cleared the harbour mouth, itself a magnificent feat of seamanship. She soon disappeared in the spray and mistiness. Five days later she returned. Her catch made record prices. Her's was the first to be landed for several days. There can have been few more testing human relationships than that between a skipper and his owner, as that story showed!

The short skirmish between Skipper Larke and his owner also tells of the same relationship. It also reveals the value which the owner placed upon a good skipper when he allowed Larko to take the smack, although he had already substituted another. I never heard how he placated the other man.

Owner–skippers, there were quite a number, with a wary eye on their bank managers. They dealt directly with their crews. They shared the same life. They had to be the toughest of owners. A good mate was as valuable to them as a good skipper was to the bigger owners.

What was there to help skipper with his many sided isolated job? Just a compass, a clock, a copy of Whitaker's Almanac and a lead line. These, I feel, would make a modern skipper turn pale.

I knew they had charts. I came across one in the junk hole of East Dean, covered in dust and tightly fastened with red tape. It seemed a matter of pride to do without it. I heard of a skipper seen using one – "There 'e wuz a measur'n th' thing with a bloody match stick". I never saw one in use.

Whitaker's Almanac gave him the tide tables which he checked with the cabin clock.

When I saw my first lead line I thought it was a spare mass of thin, rather greasy rope in a wooden box and dumped out of the way in the little boat. I only noticed the lead itself when skipper told Decky to fetch it. It was a solid cylinder of lead some twelve inches long and about two inches in diameter.

Mate and Decky

Decky cast – not dropped – it into the sea. It reached the bottom. Decky hauled it up. Skipper studied the lead and the line. I noticed, now, that it was made untidy by bits of material sticking out at regular intervals. He chatted with father for a minute or two and then, "Oi reck'n we'll drop th' trawl", he said – that is "We'll shoot".

At other times he armed – not coated – the end of the lead with that noisome yellow grease, which appeared all over the ship.

Skipper's deductions from such sparse evidence, the touches of mud, sand and so on, sticking to the armed lead, placed him in my book with Sherlock Holmes!

I managed to learn the meaning of those untidy scraps of material – two bits of leather meant two fathoms, three meant three fathoms, a piece of white cloth stood for five, a piece of red for seven, a fragment of leather, with a hole in it, marked ten fathoms. Perhaps one day I will learn why four or six fathoms were not marked and why they called the gaps thus created – "Deeps".

The mate was to skipper a kind of smack's regimental sergeant major. He was the vital link between skipper and crew. He was responsible for the smooth running of the ship. He took his full share of the work. He must be navigator and a good seaman, good enough to take skipper's place. Important, among his demanding duties, was the regular night watch – undoubtedly the toughest of all.

It stretched from tea time to breakfast the next morning throughout the trip. No matter how much or how little rest and sleep he snatched during the day, when he took a full part in the working of the ship and sharing responsibilities with skipper, there he was on deck, every night, on his own.

Skipper left as soon as the smack docked. The mate stayed to supervise tidying up and the landing of the fish. He had to be on board early enough to have the ship ready for skipper.

On settling days he had to be back on the ship to supervise and take part in replacement of equipment, to help in such activities as "tarrin' 'er bottom" after "beach'n 'er".

The mate was a share–fisherman. In good times worth while. In bad times disappointment – and agony for the wife – because it meant being in debt to the ship. He was certificated which entitled him to act as skipper of a tosher (a smaller smack).

Next in rank came the Third Hand. Like everybody else on board, he had to be able to turn his hand to most things – but not to take charge, except in the direst of emergencies. He was either a keen young man on his way up to mate and then to skipper or an older man "stuck with 'is lot". I have a sad memory or two of the older ones of whom I heard, "Poor ole Charlie nearly went over again this trip" – and, "'E's a gett'n past it". Like the mate he was never addressed by his job – always by his Christian or nickname.

Deck Hand, always Decky, could be a young man on his way up or an elderly failure. Nonetheless, he had to be able and prepared to take part in most

My special Decky

jobs, except navigating – and possibly to be able to have a go at that. I knew two special deckies, both about sixteen. Both I am certain would have attempted anything on board.

It is when I think of them, to me as competent as anybody on board, that I wonder how quickly and where they learned so much, most of it practical, and all of it to be nigh on perfect from the outset. My memory of the squall on East Dean reminds me that the learning and the "school" were certainly tough. Having no other school than experience, no other "teachers" than skipper and anybody who cared to give advice and a "roit tell'n orf", the complete absence of any text book, and, bearing in mind, the complexity and volume, theoretical as well as practical, both deckies had done astonishingly well by the time I knew them.

A major lesson they had to learn from the word go was self reliance – "You're on your own chum". How much more that must have borne down upon skipper! Decky could ask the others. Skipper could chat things over with his mate, but, the decision and responsibility were entirely his own.

The cook, always Cooky, comes last, only as it were, in theory. In many ways he ranked second only to skipper. He had the daunting task of satisfying the enormous appetites of three or four very physical men. I can best begin with a wonderfully expressive letter from one, safely retired.

"When we used to haul the trawl the cook was sent down to the rope room (another name for the main hold) to coil the rope and what a job it was I can tell you in heavy weather and many a time I've been pulled up right through the hatch and nearly overboard when she gave a heavy roll." Now to the cooking part of the business. Us cooks used to make 20 minute swimmers which were dumplings made of baking powder, flour and water and they were quite good if you didn't let them boil too long – many a cuff over the ear hole I've had from skipper for doing so. Then we did suet duff and jam on Sunday".

I have another letter, as evocative, from another who began as a cook – usually from thirteen to fourteen years of age!

"They used to be mending the trawl at night in the middle of the winter, cook used to hold the duck lamp so they could see what they were doing and when the old man told me to shove the shoe on I used to fly down tto he engine room to get warm. We used to make tea in these shoes and they were made so you could stick them in the boiler furnace for quickness ... I first went to sea when I was 12 $\frac{1}{2}$"! (the exclamation mark is mine).

Cooky in his galley. Note the teapot shoe and the small donkey engine attached to the boiler.

Many a time they went home in tears to mother, asking for help and recipes. She, was his teacher, his skipper his headmaster and the galley his school. "Galley" is hardly truthful. It suggests a purpose built and equipped cooking centre and not the reality of Cooky's cramped space stolen, it seemed, from the already well filled engine room. "Engine" also creates a false picture. A smack's engine "The Donkey", it's one source of power, jutted from the huge boiler which took up so much of the area. It would have fitted comfortably into a smallish packing case.

As Cooky faced his coal fired range – it would have fitted as comfortably into a medium sized one

– just above his head stretched his linen line. It was rarely free from damp tea and pudding cloths and dripping boot stockings. These flapped against his head as he went to the jutting-out coal bunker two feet or so to his left. Behind him, distanced by similarly inadequate floor space, reared that massive boiler.

The boiler provided another service almost as important to the men as it's steam. It was essential for their tea. Into it's glowing open door, as my cooky friend wrote, they "shoved" the tea making shoe.

A range of shelves and cubby holes stood nearby. They held the ship's lights, tools, rags and odds and ends. There were also the paraffin and fresh water tanks, much too near to one another and the boiler – the water was tepid and tasted of paraffin.

As a kind of recognition of safety, there were on the floor slabs – like paving stones – and a metal sheet near to Cooky's range.

The lighting at all times was dim. During the day it filtered down from the open companion way and very faintly from the cabin. At night Cooky struggled with the aid of a small light from a tiny oil lamp.

Peeling spuds. Note the huge mains'l block ready for any body to tumble over

I must add that in bad weather with the companion way tightly closed the lighting must have been less than minimal and the atmosphere increasingly noisome.

So inadequate was Cooky's "culinary equipment" that I have almost overlooked it – a saucepan, a frying pan and two baking tins.

No wonder my admiration for all cookies grows every time I think of them.

Cooky also had several other jobs. One still makes me marvel that a youngster managed to cope! To jump into the hold, at night, into complete darkness to deal with the mighty and potentially lethal warp. He had to control that thing so that it coiled regularly during the hauling, and be ready to work as freely during the next shooting.

Cooky had yet another vital duty. He had to provide at any time day or night and no matter the weather, often at very short notice, mugs of their unique brew of tea.

One crew faced the unbelievable – no tea! This was not un-expected, because that particular skipper "wuz allus mean on th' grub". This cooky, not dis-mayed, reacted with commendable spirit and inventiveness.

He baked some sea–biscuits until they were a dark brown, which solved the colour problem. When cool he pulverised them as finely as he could. "Then", he said "Oi made tea in th' ordinary way". When I asked him how they received the unique blend, "It worn't bad at all", skipper said. High praise!

He had other jobs, just as important. It was his duty to maintain the ship's lights in perfect working order and condition. He had to secure each in it's correct position at exactly the right time. He took them down and saw to it that there was enough paraffin and the wick was regular and moved readily. There must never be the hint of a smear on the glass or the brilliantly shining copper containers.

Each had it's appointed spot down below. The port and starboard lights gleamed and twinkled from either side of the mizzen mast as it passed through the cabin. The trawling light and the mast head light added a gleam or two to the gloomiest corner of the engine room between the boiler and the cabin wall.

As the ship neared the harbour Cooky took on his next job as a Mrs. Mop. With him "a tid'n" down below even Skipper kept away!

Cooks, deckies, third hands and mates had to be ready and prepared to take on everybody else's job. Father boasted that he could still make a good "plum duff".

When the powers that be realised that a number of uncertificated men were taking smacks to sea, they decided that every skipper of a big smack must have one. So back to school. The headmistress of an infants' department allowed some of them into her domain. Unwisely, her school log seems to reveal. Many used the ink wells as ashtrays. Their discipline left much to be desired.

Grandfather Macey instructed and examined them. I am sure that some passed because of his kind heart. Some candidates could not write, some not read, and some could do neither. Yet most had successfully skippered smacks. I remember Aunt Sarah's, "It's a crying shame", when she heard of one man's failure. "He's been doing it alright for a number of years". One failed because, they discovered, he was colour blind. After many a trip he had brought his back safely without being able to distinguish between the red for port and green for starboard, and, the red for danger and the green or white for safety.

I have tried to be factual – and neutral. Enthusiasm and admiration cannot create a fact. There is one, undeniable and beyond dispute, fact that their work and it's conditions honed five men in a big smack, four in a tosher, into an efficient team with skipper in unchallengable control.

If any sceptic needs proof he has only to list their problems, their dangers, their simple ships little changed since the days of Drake, their primitive equipment and then try to imagine himself a smacksman.

"You must lay aside your rose tinted glasses", they accuse me of seeing everything lovely when I look back to my early days. The criticism, for that is what it really is, comes from those using late twentieth century glasses tinged with modern politics, sociology and psychology. They see the men, almost as did their contemporaries, as "bloody fools" to put up with such a job for such paltry rewards.

There was no possibility of the average person on land getting to know much about the sea man. They knew his life was dangerous, tough and dealt with smelly fish. They knew he worked away from home. Most of them, biased by the unfair and out dated reputation of "half civilised toughs" from the far off fleeting days, dismissed them to a very lowly grade in Lowestoft society, unaware of or ignoring the prosperity they brought to the town.

The same accusation cannot be levelled against J. B. Priestly who met the Hull men on his "English Journey", published in 1934, four years before father retired.

"The trawler crews were still a race apart, perhaps the last of the wild men in this tamed island of ours, capable of working day and night without food and sleep, when the occasion demanded it, and then also capable of going on the booze with equal energy and enthusiasm. They are intensely loyal to their skippers ... but do not care a damn for anybody or anything else. I could not help thinking why somebody does not give us a film about these men, slaving and roaring away just round the corner, as a change from anachronistic Wild West heroes or gangsters gutter rats. The existence of such fellows, not yet forced into the dreary pattern of cockney clerks and shop walkers. Let us for sanity's sake preserve some variety in our manhood".

Who could cavil at Winston Churchill speaking in the House of Commons of fishermen at war: *"They are not men trained to war, they are fishermen ... for their courage, for their resolution, for their service they have rendered – and for the resource they have shown, I invite the House of Commons in this resolution to thank them"* ... and it did, with acclamation.

I have been asked "Could you pick out a smacksman, say in the street?" My answer is a very hedged, "Perhaps".

Did they fit into the fictionalised image created by television and fiction – big, muscular, exuding a boisterous masculinity? If they existed I never met them.

I met Owen Martin, young, virile, athletic and attractive but, like his brother Skipper Frank, quiet and soft spoken. I met Decky of Crimson Rose, young, active, strong, louder than Owen but otherwise far from the television image.

I think of Larko, Orso, Stumpy, Skipper Wales. No doubting their masculinity! No resemblance here to the popular image. Father fits in not at all. Uncle Bob was the only one I can remember who had a touch of the hale and hearty. Stumpy had it a bit more strongly.

Did they exude physical well being? They needed it. As for that generally accepted sign of good health, a tanned face, Frank Martin, Larko and Stumpy, almost as healthy as anybody, were pallid, especially Skipper Frank's, when compared with mine after a hot summer with tennis, cricket and swimming. Father's was more tanned. I was disappointed to read it described on his Royal Navy health certificate as just, "Fresh".

So anybody looking at photographs from the past expecting to see the fictional seaman, must be prepared for disappointment. Take height. I can only remember one tall smacksman. He stooped! Few, very few, were above five feet seven or eight and I have my own pet explanation for this!

It's based on the fact that any smacksman above that height faced cracked and sore heads and headaches. On deck the mizzen and main boom could give a nasty crack. Especially the main so much the more massive and with it's great main sheet block. A blow from that as it swung over, with a crash that often shook the ship, would mean a cracked skull or, at the least, a badly bruised one. As for the mizzen boom, even I in my pre–teenage days had to watch it.

When a tall man, with his arms usually longer than the others, and so stretched further over the rail to haul in the nets, he became more vulnerable to a freak wave. Like all the others he had just the few square inches of the knees of his leather thigh boots for safety.

A tall man below must again watch out or risk permanent headache or worse. He turned left at the bottom of the companion way, had to look out for the top of the cabin doorway an inch or more too low. Stretching across the cabin ceiling were the heavy deck beams, again too low for him. Even my teenage head brushed them! As for the bunk which even I found cramping – impossible.

So I suggest that over the years kindly Nature evolved the smacksman with fewer inches.

Did the average smacksman only medium in height resemble in any way the fictional picture? In build they were as varied as those in any other job. Larko, Frank Martin, and certainly Cooky on East Dean and others were spare in build.

Father, Uncle Bob, Skipper Chambers, Stumpy and others, approached the Lowestoft's "as broad as 'es long" standard.

They all, no matter their build, were strong – again they had to be. Frank Martin's strength was phenomenal.

I saw him grasp one end of the anchor bar, solid iron, and about four feet long. He slowly and steadily raised it to the vertical. He held it there. He as steadily lowered it. I can see him at a party in our house, after much persuasion, placing a walnut in the palm of one hand. He squeezed. He opened his hand. The shell was crushed as if hit by a hammer. After more encouragement he placed two brazil nuts side by side in the palm of one hand. Again he squeezed. He opened his hand. One nut was cracked.

Decky of East Dean proved his strength as he almost made good his boast that he could hoist the mizzen by himself. This was a clumsy sail, the second largest on board, with a long, heavy gaff. One young man "a 'aul'n on 't!"

When I was a boy I loved it when Uncle Bob swung me on to his shoulder in one exhilarating sweep, as if I were a feather – my nickname then was Tubby.

Every man on board made so little of lifting the massive trawl beam, made more ponderous by the weight of the two large iron trawl heads at each end, together with the pull and weight of heavy ropes and massed netting.

During shooting they – three men – lifted all of this straight up from the deck above the rail and dropped it into the sea.

Hauling was more arduous. Bending well over the side as the beam came near enough, they lifted it out of the water, up to the level of the rail. This was an upward haul of about three feet, which increased and decreased as the smack rolled and their burden went with the waves.

I am still puzzled by seemingly frail Cooky of East Dean. Where did he store his strength which in the semi–darkness of the hold, won him his battle with the dripping warp, with a very decided will of it's own?

Others of their many daily trials of strength come to mind. Like Decky dashing up and down the net bag of fish, in the sea rushing and swirling by. The many times when two or three, with their unique "Hoip! Hoip!", tightened even further the topsail halyard which stretched some fifty feet above their heads. There is Larko swinging a basket laden with wet fish.

Then father at home. "Daddy! Do be careful! You don't know your own strength!" I cannot remember how many times I heard mother's lament as she watched father "playing" with us. I can see him having fun with my younger brother Frank who always came back for more.

We are in our large front room. Frank happily charging at father. He defends himself. Frank, a sturdy ten year old, comes at him again. Father meets him. Frank stumbles helplessly across the wide room up and over a high back four seater settee and lands in a heap behind it. "I only touched him!", he explains.

If any one thing marked a fisherman it was his hands. Not so much their size, or shape, although their fingers tended to be stubby. They were muscle bound with skin resembling tough, worn, smooth suede. With most of them their grip was almost a hand slide, almost over before it began. No fictional hand grip of the tough muscular he–man of the outdoors. Very disappointing! I wonder what treatment would have been needed after a full grip from Skipper Martin!

The smacksmen seemed to be embarrassed by the conventional handshake. Particularly so when accompanied by the usual, "How do you do?". Father always met it with , "How's y'self?". The handshake was not their thing. Their fingers muscle bound, and inured to the handling of thick ropes were probably unable really to grip a few limp fingers.

I remember the toughness of father's typical smackman's fingers when our heavy, iron kettle boiled furiously on the open coal fire in our sitting room. Whilst we were searching for a thick cloth for protection against the hot handle, "Let me do it", he said. With his bare fingers he lifted it off and gripping the handle firmly poured the boiling water into the tea pot. When two large brilliantly glowing pieces of coal fell from that same blazing fire he picked them up from the hearth rug and calmly replaced them and carried on reading his "Pink'n".

Father faced and overcame a grip crisis at sister Vera's rather "posh" wedding reception. A mug of Cooky's tea he could handle. With a small, dainty and fragile cup he faced defeat. That "darn'd silly handle" was impossible for his fingers. He dared not grip it too hard. "We smacksmen don't give in", so he buried the whole cup in his hands. He raised it to his lips. His rather bulbous nose intruded. He tilted his hands and cup. In two loudish sips, he emptied it.

"You'll wear gloves", mother had decided when the wedding was planned weeks earlier. Father's face said all. I agreed with his unspoken reaction. A smacksman with gloves!! What would his crew say? I tried unsuccessfully to visualise father's smacksman's hands in them – once he got them on! "You can't let Vera down on her wedding day", she said, "You know you've got to take her down the aisle". I treasure the reactions of the man in the shop as father, totally uncooperative, struggled with glove after glove with always the danger of a split. "They'll do", he said firmly.

The wedding car arrived. "Where are your gloves?", mother said. How well she understood her man! "I've split one of them", father said, "practising getting it on". "No time to do anything about that now", mother said. "You'll have to carry that one". Father performed admirably. "Where are your gloves now", said mother as we all arrived at the reception. After a quick, suspicious kind of fumbling, "Darn it!", said father complacently, "I must have left them in the church. Shan't need them in a hurry". Mother, wisely admitting defeat, said nothing.

Another thing which marked a Lowestoft smacksman on shore was the fisherman's roll, as mother called it, which affected his walk. It is not easy to describe.

It began just above the ankles as he stepped forward. It travelled through the body up to and including the shoulders and it gave to his walk a kind of roll. This, if very marked, hinted at very minor tipsiness. It surely had to be so after years of a adapting to the many movements of a small ship. I, after only a few days, walked as if I were well and truly "over the eight".

I can clearly see four elderly smacksmen enjoying a chat. It is Sunday morning with the market it's usual quiet, deserted self. They are at the far end clearly silhouetted against a sun lit sky, adding quite a theatrical touch.

They are deeply engaged in a conversation which I cannot hear. One breaks away. He slowly rolls a few steps there and back. Another does the same, then another until everybody has moved. They come together again. Each takes another walk in turn, but not in the same order. As this continued I noticed that they all moved away for the same number of steps and back again. I also noticed they could stand still only for a short while, and each for roughly the same length of time – I thought about this.

A smack's deck is never still. If you try to stand for any length of time you'll tumble. In it's confined space you can only walk so far there and back, which led to their wry quip, "Three steps 'n overboard".

I noticed it again on a Saturday afternoon with a skipper patiently waiting for his wife inside the shop nearby which dealt with "women's things". A place to which any smacksman would have to be dragged by his capstan or a herd of elephants.

His was a repeat performance. He moved forward and back a similar distance and in the same manner as the market four with one very big difference. He was alone and vulnerable to any passing smacksman. So he looked neither to the right, nor to the left, but slightly downwards, so avoiding the eyes of all passers by.

After what seemed a long time to me – probably eternity to him – his wife came out. She carried a well filled paper bag. She clearly wanted to show him the contents. He would have none of it. He quickly pushed his arm through her's. They hastened away in a manner which strongly suggested that, even after many years, she had not mastered the knack of walking with a man with a fisherman's roll.

I cannot recall much in the way of clothing which marked the smacksman on shore. His carefully kept "Sunday go t' meet'n suit", rarely worn, was usually navy blue. Some wore dark green. Others, younger and more daring turned to brown. Some even with a faint stripe. They preferred the double breasted jacket. Some, a few of the young and daring, sported bell bottomed trousers. Boots were always black, lace ups. Again it was the youthful and adventurous who sported pointed toes and curved, slightly higher heels. Shirts were generally white and, even with their best suit, they were often worn without the collar – detachable in those days. To offset this and to hide the shine of the brass headed stud they wore a neck wrapper. This could be black or any other dull colour. Without a single exception, that is in my memory, they wore the flat cap. The way in which he wore it could be quite revealing of the man.

Father was persuaded to have a new suit of faint herring bone patterned cloth in quite a pale grey. An outstanding act of sartorial courage in such an almost fanatically closed world as the smacksman's. We dared him to wear it when he went to The Office for the next settling – and he did. I tried and failed to get him to tell me the reactions of the others. Then dawned "the" day.

I am not overstating it's significance! It was the day when a smacksman – father – came to Lowestoft market in a trilby, a soft felt, stylish hat worn by landsmen of many classes – but never by a smacksman. Much, much later it was suggested to him that the trilby was now "fit for the smack". He accepted this challenge, but not before he had manhandled it severely and reduced it to a kind of dishevelled cowboy hat fit for a scarecrow. Now with little or no resemblance to it's former elegance, it served him well on board. "It doesn't blow off too easily", he conceded.

During my childhood, any semblance of a typical sea rig for smacksmen gradually went. However one article lingered on, the nigh on universal tan coloured jumper, loose fitting, crew necked, below the waist garment in a kind of sail cloth. Some continued with trousers of very

tough, heavy, soft textured cloth, called duffel, often with flap flies secured by two top buttons instead of the usual fly button type. On their feet they had thick stockings blue or more often a creamy light grey, and knitted at home. At sea these were frequently replaced by the great boot stockings in a creamy, greasy wool. They reached well into the "crotch" ready for those, to me, gigantic sea or crotch boots. Mighty things they were. Of thick leather, shaped at the top and with heavy leather soles at least one inch in thickness which father said, he had "riveted" on! From time to time father's came home; they looked so grotesque as he arrived with them dangling low from his shoulders and swaying as he walked.

He stood them for at least a day filled to the brim with water. He emptied them and left them on mother's linen line which sagged dangerously under their great weight. Finally, deemed dry enough, he coated them liberally with linseed oil.

I fell to temptation on the day he left them in the scullery. I drew up a chair. They well topped the seat on which I stood. I put a toe into one yawning black hole. I slipped and fell, helpless, with one leg

The trilby!

56

Father climbs - *in his massive
leather sea-boots*

painfully up to my thigh and the other dangling outside. There I stayed until rescued by mother.

How did they move easily and safely about the slippery decks in those great objects? How could they move freely at all? I once watched father climb the rigging and "hump up" the highly varnished top mast to mend a block in those cumbersome things.

They also wore heavy, leather wellingtons. For heavy weather they put on the sou'wester and the oily frock, both shapeless, oilskin protectors from which, rain, spray and sea water speedily departed. Both worked well.

Their oily frock was one of the ultimate garments in shapelessness. It only fitted where it touched around the neck and the wrists but, at the wrist it was lined with a rough serge like material. Constantly wet and damp throughout the winter it irritated the skin. From this developed the dreaded salt water boils. The frock slipped over the head and shoulders. It had no buttons or fastenings and so no seeping holes and tiny openings.

Storm gear

The sou'wester made of similar oily material worked as effectively. It had a short peak in the front and a much longer one at the back. It's lining was of rough serge similar to that in the oily frock.

Father, teased about his increasing baldness, ran his fingers through the healthy growth immediately above his ears and at the back of his neck. "Look at this!", he said, "I've told you before – it's the rub of the sou'wester!".

The oily frock also came home for servicing. Father stretched it on the back garden concrete and scrubbed it with a stiff yard broom. He left it to dry, then hung it on the washing line with it's arms extended by the linen pole. He thoroughly coated it with linseed oil. It swayed like a demented, headless scarecrow for several days.

As my teenage years approached and departed so did any recognisable style of sea clothes. In came the era of "Things fit for the dustbin, but still serviceable". As father said, "They look alright" and to my eyes they looked alright in them – he looked more at ease than in his best suit.

I can recall the garnsey, heavy, warm and often knitted by hand, with pure wool, at home.

They had a crew neck shaped collar. A few were patterned.

I remember Granny Finch's flashing, non–stop, steel knitting needles producing garnseys. She rarely used a pattern, or, if she had one, she never looked at it. She also knitted long boot stockings to be worn with the sea boots. She added enough at the top of each to form a generous over turn. She used large balls of whitish, oily wool she called "ob". As she worked she chatted leaning slightly forward as her apparently unregarded needles glittered and clicked.

Those sea boot stockings were marvellous for Christmas. Their cavernous space must have given Father Christmas a bit of a headache in our seven stockinged house.

"Don't they speak quietly, almost softly", my wife said. We were sitting at a table enjoying a fish and chip supper at our local shop. We had not long come to Suffolk and this was the first time she had listened to a group of locals. They were queuing for their evening newspaper wrapped treat. I was surprised. Even as a Suffolk man this was something I had never noticed. I listened with her. She was right! Here was a possible explanation for the few orders at sea, I probably never heard the others!

The men I knew held a natural tight rein on their tongues. The only one I can remember at all voluble was Stumpy James. His was spasmodic and worth listening to. Father's rein with seven boisterous, healthy youngsters about the place, must have turned to steel, as this story shows.

It began early one morning after he came in dog tired and went straight to bed. My older brother Victor and myself got up at half past seven to get ready for school – this happened in Cornwall so we faced a four mile walk. An argument ensued. Our voices raised. A faint growl from above, "Stop that". After a few minutes silence the argument broke out again, louder. A somewhat louder growl from above and we just made out "If that happens again I'll come down to you". Unfortunately I accidentally shattered the silence that followed – Victor pushed me. I fell against the heavy set of fire irons followed by a terrifying clang as metal met the stone of the hearth. I saw father in night-shirt enter, barefooted, which explained why we had not heard his approach. He aimed a mighty kick at my rear and missed. No words and in this eerie silence he returned to bed. We heard nothing further until mother, at least twelve months later, told all. "When he came back I could see he was in agony. He got back into bed without a word. Later he told me that when you dodged his kick he caught his big toe on the table leg". That was a very solid, wooden country style kitchen table! I felt for him! "Yes", she said, "he still feels it at times". Even all that failed to make father "blast off".

Even Skipper Larko, angry as he was – and scared too – because his ship had teetered on the edge of disaster when Decky failed to see that approaching squall. Even with every reason to behave otherwise he stood still! He spoke quietly! His nose at times almost touched Decky's. Every barbed word went straight home.

He had a voice! When he yelled "Trawl–o–o!" the men soon tumbled on deck. This could have been habit because they flattered me by responding as smartly to my treble.

As to their Suffolk accent, it was – and still is – almost impossible both to describe and to imitate. it still defeats actors. I will not attempt to say why! I will hazard a guess – it is more a variation in pitch and speed, with an attractive hint of flatness than a dialect and, of course, it's quietness and it's slight rise at the end of a sentence.

They frequently used the present instead of the past, as, "I see 'im yesterday". They tended to drop aitches and g's as in "'im", "'er" and "'ome"; and "runn'n", "laugh'n". Their "i" as in "I'm" and "time" moved towards "Oim" and "t'oime". If it were simpler to discard or add a syllable or a letter or two they did so. Lowestoft became "Low'stf", Happisburgh became "Haze'br'" and mainsail changed to "mains'l" and topsail to "torps'l", pneumonia came out as "peumonia". Another characteristic was their placing of emphasis on words with two and more syllables – very firmly and with a hint of a drawl on to the first, so strongly at times the second syllable almost went. Their town became "LOWstf". Mainsail came out as "MAINs'l" and northward as "NOR'rd". At the end of a phrase these tiny explosions had an upward lilt.

Almost to a man, and a boy, they enjoyed a "fag" or a "gasper" or a "coffin nail". The last was the woodbine – $\frac{1}{2}$ penny for 10 in a green coloured open ended paper packet. There were others a bit more expensive, Wills Gold Flake, B.D.V. and so on. Father favoured Players Navy Cut. He probably saw himself in the very macho naval seaman pictured on the packet.

Apart from a snooze, a cigarette was his one way to relaxation. They took up very little space in the pocket. They were easy to light. Even in a high wind there was always somewhere a small sheltered spot.

Some "rolled their own" which became widely used with the coming of the little roller machine.

There were markedly fewer pipe smokers. Perhaps it was more expensive. Certainly in a high wind it was much more difficult to light, and to keep alight. There was always the risk of hot ash in the eyes. There were perforated barrel caps to deal with this. They carried tobacco tins and on the highly polished lid they often scratched a picture of their smack.

Fewer still "chewed", the constantly moving tiny bulge in their cheeks fascinated me. They had their shiny tins to contain their "twist". When I saw my first sample I thought it was the liquorice which we bought for one farthing a strip. I quickly learned that it's taste was horribly different when I rashly succumbed to a chewer's – "Come on – be a man – It can't d' y' no 'arm". He sliced off a tiny bit – I believe it was called "a quid". I put it in my mouth. It was hard and tasteless at first. "Go on", he urged, "Y' got t' chew 't". I began. Just one bite. If I had not immediately spat it over the side I should have been violently sick. I can still see the brown stream from the chewers lips. "Over the side!. Not on the deck!" It made such an unpleasant, indelible stain. It showed on those with the heavy moustache of their day. (I cannot recall a bearded smacksman).

Third hand, pipe smoker

They had a kind of genius for apt and often clever nicknames. I have already spoken of "Orso" Osborne, "Larko" Larke, and "Stumpy" James. My father was "Finno" Finch. We called the Norfolk people "Norfolk Dumplings". They replied with "Suffolk Pea Bellies". The smack with a totally unexpected classical name of "Meum et Teum" became "Mum and Tum".

Some, like "Orso", "Larko" and "Finno", and even "Mum and Tum" are readily understood.

Possibly I can make an intelligent guess at "Long" for the tall ex–smack owner, "Jumbo" for the massive Howard, "Tiny" Turrell, "Shrimp" Finch and perhaps "Tosher" Moore. "Dadger" Long, "Dusty" Miller and "Dusty" Rhodes and perhaps "Goose" Elton are obvious. "Oive got'm" puzzled me until I learned they used it for the man who shouted it as he peddled his "cure alls". How did they arrive at "Bimbo" Mullins, "Spot" Hughes, "Wiffy" Peck, "Prince" Beamish, "Tarsh" Fisher and "Elijah"? What brought on that last one? Perhaps I may be allowed to give a laurel to "Bible Thumpers" for those who got religion badly and "Black Widders" – rather unkindly – for nuns. "A Gut Starver" for a skipper who economised too rigidly on a crew's food was certainly descriptive as well as critical.

They often turned a neat and telling phrase like, "'E ain't done no 'arm", for "He's not done badly" – "Oim a jogg'n along", for "my health is quite good, thank you" – "As broad as 'es long" for "He's got very wide shoulders". One of the best had a hint of poetry and is so descriptive of life at sea on a smack, from a letter already quoted, "As we clear th' pier 'eads all friendships cease". So much more attractive and telling than "your'e on your own chum". When I asked him about father and son, brother and other close relations, "They're worse", he said.

They took on, usually successfully, everything their job threw at them. Most made it look so simple that I foolishly believed "I can do it". It took me time to realise three things about a smacksman's work. It was far from easy. It was complex. That it had to be mastered almost at once.

These must have terrified a boy of twelve to fifteen. A young cook had to cook at once. He was expected quickly to be generally useful. To know such things as starboard from port, the names and positions of the sails, the names of the parts of the trawl and on and on through his first day. He had to learn that mistakes were always dangerous. Turn to starboard instead of port, meant crash into the quayside or another smack. Free the wrong rope and a sail crashes down.

It would be boring to list the many tasks great and small that he had to master quickly. That they did so was clearly shown to me at the outset of my first trip.

During my first hour or so on board Crimson Rose the men just got on with getting ready. If there were any orders from father I didn't hear them. Skipper arrived and said "We'll go". Surely there must be one or two orders now. There were none.

As we made for the harbour mouth there was skipper standing at the tiller. If there were any orders I probably mistook them for casual conversation.

The same was true at sea. There were orders, necessary when they shot and hauled. I am certain there were none as they sat wherever they could to begin the gutting. Skipper, I am sure, never even thought of ordering father on deck after tea to begin his night watch. Nor did I hear a yell to Decky, after breakfast, to remind him, that it was time for him to get on deck to take over.

What a lot to learn quickly and so well as to become instinctive. Decky failed to keep his weather eye open and East Dean was in dire trouble.

I have already mentioned port and starboard, so simple but so important. I'll take halyard and sheet. The first hauls a sail, the second tightens and "sheets it home", and holds it in place. Imagine the chaos if a halyard is confused with a sheet and the sail comes hurtling down instead of being "sheeted" safely home. Each sail had it's halyard and sheet, each had it's own point of fastening, it's cleat, and this had to be so learned that he went to it instinctively in the dark or in the tension of a sudden, violent storm.

They had to learn about the handling of the sails – name, position, function, how to set, how to reef.

Turning from sails to the standing rigging. Which, as the name implies, is permanent. Here again is another collection – shrouds, ratlines, cross trees, mizzen, mast and mainmast, and so on.

The things he had to learn about rope! The word itself was rarely heard – tow rope, ground rope are the only ones I can recall. There are the many with a special name usually given from it's work. Sheet – the rope that makes tight. Lanyard – the rope that hauls. Painter – the rope that secures. Ratline – the rope fastened to the main shroud so forming a rope ladder called the rigging. Here is a smacksman's feeble joke. "Why is a smack a she?" – answer "Because she has stays" (a necessary support for the ship's mast as well as for a lady in those far off days).

The things they had to learn to do with ropes! Hitch, bend, belay, splice, reeve, whip, fit a becket, make a grommet, make a purchase mouse and marry and worm – many of these they had to master quickly – instance hitch, bend, lash – and beware mistakes. As for knots! They could so easily lead to bewilderment, and again the word itself was rarely used – and except for a few reef knot, granny knot.

What names some of them had! Who made them up? Running bowline, bowline on the light, stopper, nettle, becket, turks head – there were several hitches, clove hitch, timber hitch.

In later years, fascinated since my young days, I looked up knots. I learned "spliced" they used for "getting married", as did my father. The dictionary says "it is a means of fastening two ropes together so that they can stand up to great strain without parting". Quite an old fashioned concept of marriage! It also speaks of it, "as a means of securing so that it does not break away" – old fashioned again!

The dictionary further told me of a "rolling hitch" which tightens under stress and strain and a "half hitch" much less secure.

Grandfather Macey, a knot expert, used the turks head to decorate the ends of the girdles of coats mother was making for my sisters. It is the most attractive and the most difficult to make – the Encyclopaedia Britannica had to give up trying to describe how to create it!

The young man had to learn much about fish. Probably at his very first hauling he had to learn to distinguish between prime and non prime. How to recognise a sole, a slip, a plaice, a dab, a whiting, a haddock and so on. One name would puzzle him as it did me when I first saw it. They called it "roker" – in the fish and chip shop it was known as skate!

The bewildering list facing the young smacksman grew when faced with the trawl – the beam, trawl head, bridles, ground rope, cod end and the nettle. As with knots he had to learn their purpose and how to make them. He had to master shooting and the hauling. Later on he would have to learn when and where to shoot, how long to leave it down and when the cod end was ready for the hauling.

He had to learn that there was a right way and a wrong way of doing things.

A young smackman I knew chose the second, and paid the price, when something went wrong with the large block at the end of the main boom. He was asked to see to it. He could turn a fish trunk upside down and stand on that – the right and safe way. He could leap on to the always damp and slippery rail only a few inches wide – wrong but showy. He chose the second. The boom swung over sharply and knocked him overboard. They tried to save him and failed. He had broken the smacksman's unwritten law, "Do everything carefully", and lost his life.

Mending the trawl at night under the weak and wavering light of a flickering, smokey naptha lamp! The dog fish had been at work. The gaping holes they made in the nets! They must be well and truly mended to leave the trawl ready for the next shooting, perhaps straight away. An hour at least of essential sleeping time lost because of "them bloody dawg fish". All of this in the middle of winter.

Mending the trawl was a highly skilled and demanding job in daylight. As usual they made it look so easy that I had a go. Father handed me "the needle", a flat thin strip of wood about ten inches long and three inches wide with one end pointed, there was an opening cut down the middle. I managed to thread it with the yellowy new twine – I had to stop it from sliding out by using my thumb. With needle at the ready I was shown how to bring the two sides of the hole together and to hold them firmly with the thumb and first finger of the left hand.

"All you have to do now", father said, "Is to twist the needle, push the twine through and pull ... It's easy!" Yes, to him. I found I failed to twist soon enough and when I pulled the knot came undone. My thumb and finger were not strong enough to hold the edges of the hole together. I gave up. The only sign of his beautiful mending was the lighter colour of the new twine.

So much to learn and they were well and truly thrown in at the deep end as I discovered on a beautiful sunny morning.

East Dean was bowling merrily along under a steady breeze with Decky on watch. He stood at the tiller clearly at peace with the world. I, also at peace, sat on an up–turned fish trunk peeling spuds for Cooky – their plop into the bucket by my side was the one alien sound.

Suddenly, I was following my clattering bucket down the steeply sloping deck towards the scuppers flooded with foam streaked sea rushing aft. Fortunately I crashed into the cabin top and stayed there. I was sure that with just a tiny increase in the tension a sail would split, a mast splinter, a rope snap or East Dean would turn over.

Just as quickly the tension went. East Dean was now sailing merrily along under a steady breeze. Skipper Lark, all tousled, appeared on deck. He faced Decky almost nose to nose.

There came another storm, a verbal one, as violent as the one just gone. Skipper didn't shout.

He just stood there. I could only hear an occasional word. Just as suddenly this storm ended. Skipper went below.

I felt so sorry for Decky and thought that skipper had gone a bit too far. Later I said as much to father. To my surprise he disagreed with me. "Skipper did the right thing", he said.

He would have been blamed for any loss of life, or accidents or damage to or the loss of his ship. "There must have been something to see as a squall like that was coming". As he spoke I remembered a small cloud, like a black, fuzzy cricket ball, racing across the sky just before the squall struck. "This'll do him good", father said, "He's got to learn to keep his weather eye open". Do him good! He's got to learn, so the weather and the ship were his school. Skipper the mate and the more experienced smacksmen his teachers. I've never seen or heard of any text book - I think of Skipper Woulnough and the six skipper brothers all of whom could not read.

All those skills, experiences and lessons yet they were only part of that vital extra something which I can only call Seamanship.

The nearest I have ever come to understanding it came from studying the instrument panel of a modern trawler, it told wind force, wind direction, air pressure. Others reported to skipper the depth of the sea, the presence or otherwise of fish down there. Yet another told him of the weather prospects, where the changes were coming from and whether they would be good for fishing. Another linked him with help and advice by means of a ship to shore telephone.

In his letter father spoke with surprise when he saw the beginning only of these changes. Collars and ties on ready for shore and home immediately their ship docked. Somebody else to do the tidying up and not expected to tread the deck for the next forty eight hours!

If he and the other smack skippers and mates could see that panel and those switches, I am sure they would have the same reaction - with different wording - "Wot are all them gadgets for? We didn't 'ave 'm, 'n we didn't do too badly" - and, I will add, "We must've 'ad 'm all in our 'eads". Which is true - they didn't need them. They were seamen.

They did the same job in smaller ships, under sail, and with minimal equipment, ridiculously inadequate compared with the abundance at hand for the moderns.

One gadget they would not have welcomed - the ship to shore telephone. They didn't want blokes at home, who probably had never worked on a smack and sat on their "arse all day, a tell'n them wot t'

do". Their belief in themselves was prodigious and well founded!

A skipper caught by a dense fog, "couldn't see 'is 'and in front've 'is face!", in the difficult approach to Lowestoft harbour, beset by shallows, and tricky gaps. He made home by the lead line, equivalent to finding his way blindfolded.

Grandfather Finch, they told me, could sail back to where he had caught plenty of fish, "'n 'e worn't th' only one".

Another snippet proves how intimately they knew the waters over which they sailed. I noticed as we moved over the same testing approach to harbour that the sea was steadily becoming more and more sandier. Were we in danger of grounding I asked skipper? "N'th'n t' worry about", he said, "There's a lot a sand down there 'ere abouts".

A seaman told me two stories about my father which help to explain what I call seamanship.

They took place at Padstow in Cornwall under conditions as different as possible from Lowestoft. The wide open Atlantic, as against the enclosed North Sea with it's sandy shores, as against the rocky cliffed ocean coast. The problems entering Lowestoft harbour are almost simple when compared with those of Padstow – and especially in the stormy conditions of these two stories. The ship, Crimson Rose, was built for and crewed by men experienced in North Sea fishing. Even to get to Padstow she had to sail from Lowestoft through the German submarine and mine infested North Sea and English Channel.

A ship approaching Padstow enters the very wide mouth of the River Camel completely open to the Atlantic. It is bedevilled and split into two channels by an enormous rock - aptly called "The Doom Rock". The two mile stretch to Padstow has high rocky cliffs to starboard and sandy beaches to port. The dangers were underlined in those days by the constant presence of a steam life boat, it's readiness proclaimed whenever I saw it by a whisp of steam. The tide runs very swiftly and very strongly.

I can still see my boots sweeping away as I paddled, concentrating upon my model yacht. I ran hard and long to rescue them, with the water rising up to my knees. I can also clearly recall the massive Padstow ferry boat, rowed by one man - or his daughter! - forced to land hundreds of yards from it's appointed spot by a mixture of tide and current.

The harbour itself is cunningly placed under the shelter of great, high rocks. It's narrow entrance, between two stone jetties, is parallel to the opposite shore, which means a perfectly judged right angled turn to starboard - or else a collision with a jetty or the ugly rocks adjoining it.

So, altogether, a demanding job for the stranger even in daylight. These episodes took place at night - in stormy weather. I clearly recall both because the Atlantic sprayed our house which stood more than two miles from "The Doom Rock".

The date is 1916. Father had gone to Padstow because of the loss of men and smacks from the German mines and submarines. We followed him as soon as he found a house. It was in Rock, a tiny hamlet opposite Padstow on the far north bank of the very wide estuary of the River Camel. This meant that we fully felt the moods of The Atlantic.

I remember vividly that dreadful winter's night when father was making for home driven by a powerful following wind. I heard the complete story from a sea faring, very close friend. He crossed the Doom Bar safely. Protected by the tall rocky cliffs to starboard Crimson Rose swept towards Padstow. The wind changed. The rocky cliffs were now dangerous. He had hugged them closely before the change came. He beat away against the wind. No simple task in a gale. He still faced much of the two miles to Padstow. He knew well, after several months experience, the opposite sandy shore of the Camel estuary. He decided to beach Crimson Rose at a spot from which he could float her at high tide the next day. So ... he grounded her!

"Don't make a lot of noise", mother said the next morning as I came down to breakfast. "Daddy's upstairs. He came home a few hours ago. He's very tired". Later he enjoyed a late breakfast and left, "I've got a job to do", he said. He returned later. He said nothing about his job! He had refloated Crimson Rose. Taken her to Padstow. Sold his fish. After a few minor repairs she went to sea again.

Similar horrific weather with similar dangers and problems dominated the second story. The heavy storms which had driven Crimson Rose towards Padstow and over the Doom Bar changed as before. Now they blew against her, which meant slow progress and a lengthy and searching test of father's seamanship and his crew. When he finally reached harbour with the heavy wind and the Camel raging like an open sea intensified the problem of it's entrance and increased the danger of crashing against the two solid jetties which formed it. Against the high wind and the swirling river urging him onwards he had to judge to perfection both the direction and the timing of his sharp turn to starboard. He made harbour. "Never been done before", said the locals. He sold his fish and went to sea.

A similar gale raged through two days and nights. Fortunately father was at home. Well after dark on the second night we heard the life boat rocket. Somebody was in trouble. I thought of the life boat and it's crew. The next day I saw on the beach a large object shaped like a half ball. Later our local policeman came and ordered us to report to him if we found any others. "They're important. They're all rubber".

Father said he must get to Padstow. He ignored our opposition and left for the ferry. He returned soon. It wasn't working. The water too rough he said. He arranged for the local carrier to take him to Wadebridge more than ten miles away. From there he would take the train to Padstow. The driver agreed to take we children because he passed near to our school - saving us our usual four mile walk. Our pleasure became pride as the other children gasped when we stepped down from a quite impressive horse drawn carriage. Father promised to pick us up when he came back. We waited a long time after school, but, we walked home. Father had managed to get a message to mother. He had gone to sea.

These stories went the rounds of the pubs and the Padstow fish market and received quite high praise from the locals as sparse with their compliments as the Lowestoft fishermen. I still wonder if the seamanship of father and his crew would have worked as well, or better, if his panel of gadgetry had been in front of him instead of in his head. The modern skipper must be a different kind of seaman. I must plead guilty of bias towards Orso Osborne's "iron ships wooden men". Was he a very old man looking back through thickly rose tinted glassed?

I must include two incidents which show how wrong I was to think that their work were so simple that I could do parts of them.

"Steering" was one. So when father said, "I'm going below. Do you think you can take the tiller?" Could I? Of course I could! I'll show him I vowed!

Here I must outline the setting. It was near midnight on a wonderful autumn night. King herring had arrived off Lowestoft. We were out to catch him in our own ship, Our Boys, a sixteen footer long shore boat. About a third of a mile of drift net stretched away from us. It hung vertically from it's many round corks to entrap the herrings swimming just below the surface.

I picked out one star of the host floating above our bows. I'll swear my eyes never moved from it. They watered. I may have blinked once or twice. Suddenly, "What d' you think you're doing!" It was father shouting in some alarm, "You'll be

"Our Boys" - our long-shore boat

fouling our nets". I looked over the side. I was steering straight for them. He quickly corrected my course - but - more was yet to come when Father decided to haul.

There was no cumbersome trawl needing a capstan. So we steadily pulled in by hand the light weight net into which the herrings were entrapped by their gills. I soon noticed that too many of mine were slipping free and swimming away - rarely did I see father losing one - so this, too, was not as easy as I thought. I imitated him perfectly, but, too many still fell back into the waves. "You'd better pick'm up and put'm into the basket", father said. Two failures in one night - both appeared so easy!

I thought sculling was easy. That is when I watched them. They sculled with one oar instead of rowing the little boat.

You had to stand, not sit, on the seat. I did that. You had to fit the one oar into a groove cut for the purpose into the top of the stern. I did that. Then, grip the handle of the oar and twist it very rapidly and very strongly so that the blade rotates like a propeller.

I began to do that. I was neither skilful enough and most certainly not strong enough. The boat rocked but did not move. I increased my efforts. I made lots of foam - and - fell off the seat. The boat had not moved.

Chapter 9

Rewards

Uncle Albert brought the word exploitation into our home. I was about twelve at the time. I listened to his arguments. I agreed with him. To my surprise, father did not. "The owner wouldn't treat me like that", he said, with childlike loyalty. Uncle Albert left rather ruffled having failed to convince him that he was badly underpaid.

Only a few weeks earlier I had tried and failed to make him accept that the big difference between the money he received for his fish on the market and the prices charged in the fishmonger's shop, only some two hundred yards away, was very unfair. Father listened, "I know all that", he said, "but I wouldn't like his job, he's got too many responsibilities". A smack skipper talking of another man's responsibilities!

I tried to convince him by comparing his lot with that of men we both knew.

"Take Gassy Cook", I said. He was a tram driver and played full back for Lowestoft Town. "He's got a nice clean job. He's got regular hours, regular wages and he's home every day". Father said, "I'd go crazy driving up and down London Road like that".

I was equally unsuccessful with several other attempts. "You're running your head against a brick wall", mother said – which makes it all the more remarkable that three years earlier, and myself three years younger, I had persuaded him to take me on my first trip!

I came across the same attitude in the cabin of East Dean as I listened to Cooky and Decky on the idea of a Lowestoft branch of the newly born Smackman's Trade Union.

As with Uncle Albert on exploitation I agreed it was a good idea – somebody to look after their wages and their jobs. Surprise again – they were strongly against it.

"If any bugger's a com'n fr'm Yarm'th a tell'n us what t'do Oil run 'm in t' th' trawl dock", Decky declared. Perhaps the fact that the delegate was coming from their ancient and hated rival had something to do with it.

Were they placidly accepting their lot like dumb animals as Uncle Albert had suggested? I cannot see any link between my fisherman friends and a pig or a horse or a bullock! I am sure it was not dumb, and docile acceptance, but, I do believe that security was the key factor.

Their's was a job in which poor results were so obvious. If continued, the sack. There were others very ready to take their place.

Their's was a tough job controlled by tough men, and life without work in those days was very tough indeed.

For many there was little else. Some said, "th' ole man made me" – others, "I just drifted into it".

I have already described how father became a smacksman. His must have been unique – to run away from home, twice, to go to sea!

A highly placed lady confessed, "Other people's family finances are a complete mystery to me". Those of a smacksmna's wife would have completely foxed her. How did my mother manage with seven children?

A skipper received two pounds a week. A mate thirty shillings (£1.50). Down and down it went through third hand, to Decky, to Cooky, from one to under a pound. Skipper following the auction of their catch doled out the stockerbait (pocket money) – a strange word, nobody seems to know where it came from or it's real meaning. I am not even sure if I am spelling it correctly. This money came from the sale of odds and ends from the catch. Skipper divided it according to rank – more or less, a bit more for a new baby or an extra large family.

"At toimes it won't too much", one said, "only sixpence (2½p!), but in them days y' c'd do someth'n' about it – a pack't a fags 'n th' pitchers".

Skipper also sorted out the "taking home fish", kept aside from the main catch, usually of non–prime fish, but in good times a plaice or two, or even a sole "slipped in". Skipper gave it out mostly "accord'n t' 'is own ideas" – usually based upon the size of the family or "a bit a illness at 'ome". Ours was always very welcome. It usually came home in a matt basket or a smacksman's white spotted red wrapper. Mother usually sent one of us with "a bit of fish" for the old lady next door, a skipper's widow.

One fish we children welcomed above all others, a latchet. that's our name for it and one it seems only used in Lowestoft. Even the specialists at the Ministry of Fisheries could not help me. A smacksman, retired to Blackpool, enquired of his local fishmonger. Yes, he had heard of it, but had never seen one. It was like a large, more highly coloured whiting. The way mother cooked it in the oven with sliced potatoes, milk and herbs! We even sopped up the "licker" with hunks of bread.

Mother's finances are still a mystery to me. Her repeated reply to my hopes of a scout uniform, a football, a bat and others, "Daddy can't afford it", said much. We fed well. She clothed us well. With father they managed to get to the cinema. She even managed to squeeze us pocket money – A farthing or a halfpenny for the seven year olds and under. A penny up to ten or eleven years of age. It is amazing what we did with a farthing. Tuppence opened up quite a world.

We lived in a working mans area, liberally sprinkled with fishing and ship building families. A narrow alley separated our small back gardens from those in the neighbouring street. A close school friend lived there. I was puzzled because his father never went to work and always seemed to be "sitting around". One day my friend proudly showed me a pair of thick woollen stockings, and a very new, very shiny pair of black boots – shoes we never wore. "A kind lady came to ours and gave them to me", he said. "What a wonderful idea", I said to mother – "A lovely pair of shiny, new boots just like Alfie's!"

"Billy!" she exclaimed. "That's charity!" No kind lady visitor for me.

I knew only of mother's struggles. From my memories of school, the homes I visited and the boys I ganged up with, I learned little.

I recall especially our football! The "ball" was often a cork from a herring net or a bundle of rags tightly bound with string. Our pitch was a strip of rough ground, or frequently between lampposts, our jackets as goal posts and with our watchful eye for our friendly enemy, the local bobby. We always seemed to be too happy to be miserable!

One boy who sat next to me in our three seater desk in Lovewell Road Senior Boys Elementary School, wore his older sister's blue bloomers, without the elastic, and her fairly high heeled shoes. We neither teased him, nor did I hear any unkind comments. His story revealed another way of becoming a fisherman.

He had to seize brief opportunities when Toddy's eyes slid elsewhere (Mr Todd was our genius of a teacher in charge of seventy two boys, yet I left him with a love of music and poetry and enough of several other subjects, including mathematics to carry me through my years at the grammar school). My companion whispered, "Oim a leav'n next week!" From a series of similar short snippets, I learned that he had taken 'The Labour Exam', his name for it, in the 3R's – Read'n, Rit'n 'nd

Hard times - "Laid Up!"

67

Rithmatic. To my astonishment he passed – he was always well below half way in Toddy's examination lists. He left. I neither saw nor heard of him again, but, what I did know, at just over thirteen years of age he was cook on a smack.

Orso Osborne spoke of his bad times, "when my ole mother was really up against it". He also told me that she brought up six other sons who, like him, became skippers. He told me how "she coped with only sixpence until father came in", (sixpence is two and a half pence today).

– and, if there's a pension at the end of it, so much the better" was ground into my generation. Unemployment was very much a dreaded spectre.

Fishing promised quite a degree of security, although without a pension. I saw what unemployment could do when the great depression of the early twenties hit Lowestoft. Father was a victim.

It seemed to change his character. He roamed the market day after day. He refused to come home

The depression of the Twenties

"She sent me first", he said, "t' the butcher for a pennuth a bones, then t' corn chandler with a penny f' some flour and t' the grocers f' a ha'p'th a bak'n powder". Then, "she sent me to 'Arry Freeman, the coal man, with an empty bucket and tuppence", which left her with a penny and a halfpenny. "With a clean pillow case and the rest of th' money Oi went t' the baker's for stale bread and stale buns 'n what you got usually depended on 'ow many brothers 'n sisters you 'ad".

Harking back to security as a partial explanation of their acceptance. "Get a good sound job for life

for meals. "You can't afford it", he said to mother. One day he was brought home – he had fainted because of hunger.

Fortunately, within a few weeks, he said to mother, "Frank Martin has offered me a job. I think I'll take it". Frank by then was an owner–skipper. He bought his smack, the lovely little Crecy, partly with the money from his war gratuity.

I am sure that father had already accepted. A tiny hint of doubt there must have been because he knew what the job really meant – basically, that two men did the work of four.

Settling time - no holiday - tarring her bottom

Two men to sail and work an isolated fishing smack. As well as working Crecy, they had a frightening list of other things – that is besides shooting and hauling, cleaning and stowing the fish. They had to navigate, to cover the watches, to cook and eat, to rest and sleep. They also faced a long list of odds and ends, like cleaning the deck after each haul, mending the nets after inevitable

father's voices and expressions, it's importance, especially when I heard father say, "I'm in debt". Mother had drawn and spent more than father's share had earned. The excess with the wages to come was then set against his share at the following "settling".

I remember particularly one Christmas, by far the worst of any other "worse" times. I heard

Settling time - chance to change the trawl beam and net

attacks by dog fish. They did it, week after week. No grumbling – father had a job, Frank Martin could face his bank manager. Father did come home and at times fell asleep even before he opened his beloved football paper, 'The Pink'un', or began his meal.

Skippers and mates were share–men. This meant that what mother drew as father's weekly wage was an advance set against his share of the hoped for profit at the next settling.

The settling was an important day, usually three each year, when father in his Sunday Suit met The Owner at The Office. Here he learned his fate and came home with a very legal looking Settling Paper, thick, very crinkly, pale blue. As I grew older I realised, from mother's and

mother say, "What can we do?" after the dreaded phrase "in debt". They talked quietly for a while, then she said, "I think it's worth a try". Father left. He was away for a long time.

When he returned he handed something to mother. She agreed with his, "He's quite a good sort really". "He" was The Owner. He had revealed under his necessary toughness that he was indeed "a good sort". We enjoyed our usual happy Christmas.

Round about twelve years of age I was allowed to look at father's settling paper, very impressive it was too. It had columns of figures. One showed fathers earnings. The other, much longer, gave the charges to be deducted – it bit drastically into his list.

Charges for food, water, general maintenance and ice I thought were fair. I was doubtful about harbour dues – When I came to percentage for the capstan! "Don't get so hot round the collar", father said. "Skipper and you", I said, "have more than paid for it over the years". Father tried soothing noises. "There's nothing to be done about it", he said.

I am still annoyed at this good example of what Uncle Albert called exploitation.

I had no excuse to "get hot around the collar" over their food. Few seamen afloat at that time were better fed. I have only to remember my "Jack–in the box" Cooky and his succession of deliveries on the morning of my first trip. There were six pieces of meat, $2\frac{1}{2}$ to 3lbs each, twelve loaves, and 1 stone of flour. Cook, retired, told me, "Y' 'ad t' be careful wi' th' bread. It got mildew too easily". Most smack's cooks were good. They had to be!

The niceties of shore and home life they did not expect and they certainly never got, nor did they grumble about it. A quick fag, "a bit a shut oiye" in the bunk or on the locker top during the day – with their expected regular mugs of tea – and, if lucky an hour or two at night even if only on the cabin floor – this was all they expected.

I am not sure if I should include the next one as a reward. To most smacksmen, no matter how kindly and thoughtful, it must at times have seemed quite a relief to sail away from the problems at home. Many a wife harassed by a child's illness, surely must have said to them as they left for the smack, "You don't know how lucky you are! You can get away from it all!" If he so wished he could indeed do so. There must have been those who shrugged their shoulders saying, "I've got to earn the money. There's nothing I can do about those things. I'll do something about it when I come in".

I remember father coming in to face the news that I was in the isolation hospital with scarlet fever and a sister was "probably sickening for it".

One smacksman returned and was told, "Y' woif's dead 'n buried" – no tact on the fish market! She died unexpectedly on the morning of his departure. Bad weather had kept him at sea for over six days.

A skipper we all knew well came in, walked home, went into his kitchen. Saw his wife with her head in the gas oven. "If only Oi'd come in earlier", he said to father.

Such a life, in such conditions with such small and by no means certain rewards could not be today. They were exploited and they had no defence against it. Yet Skipper Chambers could write "Happy Days". All those I knew had a pride in a rotten job well done. They all would have echoed the quip "In moi day wood'n ships, iron men. T'day, iron ships, wood'n men".

The very first time I took an interest in politics I was about sixteen. There was a general election. Lowestoft had a labour candidate, a conservative and a liberal – the sitting member. The conservative had a majority greater than the total number of votes cast for the other two. An astonishing result in a fishing port.

Chapter 10

The Market

After an absence of too many years I returned to Lowestoft and, as soon as possible, went to the market – quite unprepared for a shock. I knew the smacks had been replaced by highly efficient, very impressive, much bigger machines. Between me and them reared, well above my head, a closely

I do not want to enter into a controversy as to the business, security reasons and to the disregard of the feelings of so many, like myself, of the local people and summer visitors who wandered freely about the market and often boarded the ships. My anger, my disappointment at that first shock have mellowed into sadness that such freedom, such enjoyment and such a wonderful attraction, have gone.

I read recently – June 1991 – in a pamphlet listing the attractions of Lowestoft, "Organised Tours of the Fish Market", giving times, place of

The old free and easy morning market

meshed metal fence. It was just like the one to secure prisoners of war in their camp near to my wartime home. The shock increased and the similarity deepened when I was stopped at the entrance by a heavy and solid iron gate guarded by men in a military like uniform. "Where's y' permit?" they demanded. (Do I look like a criminal?) I did not know that these and those forbidding custodians existed and said so. "You can't come in without one", they said. I moved away with "Why's, Hows and Who's" crowding my mind.

assembly, and the name of the Organising Officer. Surely I am justified in bemoaning those good old days.

I sadly recall the freedoms which lasted until I left Lowestoft in 1937. I wandered, I sketched. I immersed myself in the hustle and bustle of a hectically busy market and, as far as possible, into the work of those who dealt with the fish and the ships.

Banned from the market meant I could no longer climb aboard or stand on the edge of the quay and study the ships. I could no longer look down, watch the men at work and exchange pleasantries. "'Ow are yer boiy?" with the frequent reply, "Not tew bad" – or "Fair t' middl'n. 'Ows y'self?"

I remember my first visit when I was full of worries over my first trip. Men all over the place. Hectic noise, hustle and bustle, purposeful noise, hustle and bustle. They all knew what they had to do and did it regardless.

Those noises, all new, most of them loud, came at me from all sides. A metal wheeled heavily laden fish trolley, vigorously handled by a big man in an oil skin apron, his heavy hob–nailed boots adding to the babble, screeched towards me. "Out'a moiy way!" He missed me by a mere fraction of an inch. The many noises merged into a massive onslaught.

All around me were strange sights. Fish, and fish and more fish. Fish in neat rows on the wet, puddley concrete surface. Fish in boxes quickly sealed noisily by men with heavy hammers. I saw men deal with fish, wielding large, razor sharp knives. They slashed swiftly and expertly. The many sights as with the sounds merged until they became almost meaningless.

The market was a man's world, completely. A mixture of business, custom and superstition led to, "No woman on the market and on the ships". So no wife, no fiancee, no girlfriend ever waved her man farewell from the quayside. One decky brought his bride of the previous afternoon to see him off and skipper gave him "a roit tell'n off".

One woman ignored – or defied – the banning and won acceptance as "a better man than her father". He was an owner and she his representative.

At the back of the market was an unbroken range of large windowed offices, facing and opening on to it. Each displayed a name – Podd, Painter, Barnard among them. Each was an owner and, on the whole, well respected. Above them offices – and not far above again the roof sloped gently to it's ridge and from there more steeply to an open range of supporting wooden columns. It was open on this side and at each end to every rainy or snowy wind that blew. It was somewhat dimly lit and, in the morning, hectically and noisily busy, it's not altogether level floor, wet and puddley.

I remember the herring market for it's continuing almost frenzied excitement. It seemed to shout, "Hurry, Hurry! Hurry!! – The King is only here for

Ready for King Herring

Mayhem at the Harbour Mouth

a few weeks! Make the best of it!" Hustle and bustle of the ships laden to the gunwale eager to unload and away again, each empty birth quickly filled, by an impatient competitor. It spread to the harbour mouth where the steamers crowded impatiently and noisily. Here the loaded incomers competed for a way in with those with empty holds as ruthlessly seeking a way out. Many near misses. Many noisy hooters variously signalling loudly, "I'm coming ahead", "I'm turning to port or starboard" or plain and straightforward, "Get out of my bloody way". The smoke billowing from the tall, slender funnels created a fey like light especially in late afternoon. This on the sea and on the market often lasted well into the night.

I preferred the evening market. I often went with a basket hoping for a herring or two. I quickly learned from the more experienced boys of the three ways to go about it. – Number one, ask politely of the man concentrating on a herring filled basket swinging in the air towards him, "Please will you give me one?" – not very successful, and the risk of the boot, or, "Clip around the ear". Number two, wait for one to slip from the swiftly swinging basket and fall safely away from the man, jump in and seize it – quite successful. I preferred this one. Number three – wait your opportunity, avoid the man "'n pinch one" – I skipped this, probably too scared? All in all, I was never very successful at any of the three.

I remember as clearly as anything else the phosphorescent glow of a fresh herring. A marked glow on the ceiling of our larder puzzled me until I noticed a plateful of herrings which had recently arrived. I enjoyed the same glow on the hands, arms, aprons, and boots of the men dealing with the incoming baskets. They shone beautifully and ghostly against the blackness of the evening sky. It was the same gleaming which I enjoyed in the moonlight as the waves curved before they broke on the shore.

A number of the men on board the Lowestoft drifters worked at other jobs until the herrings arrived. Some of them cycled in from the countryside – or walked. One lived in our village. When a small boy he walked with his father to Lowestoft – 20 miles away – to join his drifter. They set off very early in the morning. With his father now probably at sea he began his long walk back. With him he took some herring which he sold in the pubs or bartered for a meal. When the herrings departed his father and the many others went back to their rural jobs – until The King returned the following October.

Standing out even more clearly are the Scotch Girls, unfairly nicknamed by some as the "Scotch Moggies". I remember their skill, their endurance, their gaiety. Unlike their dour men they chatted, and chatted and chatted. They laughed and smiled incessantly, at work, in their lodgings and in the streets. I can still hear and see them on the sea front, several together, strolling arm in arm, except one or two who mixed knitting with their chatting.

Aunt Sarah "took in" Scotch girls. Some took them in, in the unpleasant meaning of the phrase. They emptied a room and almost "left them to it". Aunt Sarah made her three comfortable, and fed them well, after all their three shillings a week helped Granny Finch, a widow with five grown up sons still at home.

I was there one evening when they returned from a very long, very tiring day's work – still chatting gaily. They stayed outside on the concreted part of the back garden, this was a particularly cold east coast autumn day. They scrubbed their wellingtons and their apron in cold water with the yard broom. These they hung, dripping on the linen line. They came in to the scullery, stone floored, in their stockinged feet. They washed. No hot taps. They shared one kettle of hot water. Then they came into the warm kitchen and demolished a huge meal – of bread and marge and – fried sprats! They went gaily upstairs "to get ready" for their evening stroll. I saw them later among several others on the sea front.

These "girls", some were mothers and grey haired grandmothers, arrived with the ships – and a few on the ships. They were as an essential part of the King's retinue as the men. They gutted the millions of herrings brought in by the ships. They

"Scotch" Girls

1927
Finch

The Scotch girls

75

worked long hours under appalling conditions. I have seen fifteenth century drawings of women at work, but for a slight change in dress they are the Scotch girls.

I remember a visit to where they were working in a blistering, frost laden east coast wind, open to everything which it threw at them. They stood only a mile or so from the sea on sodden duck boards lying straight onto the muddy clay. Above them a very inadequate corrugated iron roof. In pairs they fronted large herring filled containers. Each had one barrel for the cleaned herrings and another for the offal. Grim faced overseers stood silently around. They left the women to carry the barrels, filled to the brim, and clearly very heavy, to the area where other men stood waiting to pack the fish. I watched, fascinated, as with arms bare to the elbows they plunged their left hand into the noisome mass and seized a herring. With swift plunge and twist of the knife in the right, and with no damage to the precious roe, out came the gut which sailed immediately into the offal tub. All so swift and made to look so easy. In the time I have taken to write this round about thirty bits of offal had reached it's tub. Their hands also fascinated me, not only by their amazing speed and skill, but by the sodden bandages on almost every finger and thumb – some protected past and recent cuts. Some protected the more important fingers. Surely, I thought, these must slow them down. I saw no sign of this – they dare not reveal this with those grim faced men who expected, and demanded, the correct number of thousands of gutted herrings each long, and so physically demanding day. They worked into the night under wavering oil lamps.

Still they joked, chatted. They exchanged quips with their overseers and with any spectators, especially the men.

They dressed to suit their work. A warm head scarf. Layers of wool on top, always in dark colours, several petticoats underneath. These made the thinner ones to look plump and the naturally fat ones look enormous. There were many more of the first! On their feet were thick soled leather wellingtons and at their tops peeped the turn down of thick woollen stockings. They seemed impervious to the biting cold wind. I have been told each dealt with three thousand herrings every day. I can believe that!

At the far northern end of the herring market stood a smallish, round, red brick building where they set the price per cran of the day's catch. Inside was quite spectacular. To me it seemed more an eastern temple rather than an arena for a free–for–all auctioneering, with the auctioneer as an all powerful high priest. In the centre stood a small flat stone slab. Around the slab – it strongly suggested a sacrificial altar! – ranged tiers of stone seats. Prospective buyers casually drifted in. The ceremony began with the entry of the long white coated auctioneer and his assistant, note book and pencil in hand. Two men brought in baskets of herrings and emptied them on to the top of the stone slab. Various silent men, obviously expert by expressions and gait, strolled to the samples, smelt, handled and prodded them and returned. The auctioneer began in the same rapid gabble as when he sold trawl fish, still as unintelligible to me despite the increase in volume given by the echo. The nods, winks, gestures of the competing buyers again told much to him – nothing to me– and in a few minutes he set the financial reward for those men and ships milling outside.

The fish were liberally salted, packed into barrels firmly closed by the coopers with uniquely shaped hammers. The herrings, if sold to their most important customers, the Russians, often waited three weeks or more for inspection. The cooper removed the lids. The "inspector" lifted out a herring or two, bit and tasted it, I wonder how many throughout his inspection. If proved satisfactory the cooper banged home the lid. More than several days passed before the customers ate them! We were told that the Russian peasants drank the liquid as well.

A glut of herring brought an alarming drop in the returns on the catches. Some were dumped and some sold to farmers as manure. During one such crisis we could smell them from a field, on which they were spread, which adjoined our school football pitch.

After those few hectic weeks, King Herring left on the next stage of his mysterious journey southwards. He passed through the English Channel towards a spot where he as mysteriously vanished, to re–appear to the north of Scotland and so begin his puzzling journey southwards again, re–appearing off Lowestoft as it did the year before and the year before that, back and back into history.

The herring market for the next eleven months or so became it's familiar echoing self. The strange Scottish boats with unfamiliar registration initial initials like B.F. for Banf, L.K. for Lerwick sailed away some to follow and attack King Herring on his pilgrimage southwards. Some Scots Girls followed them, others went home. The Lowestoft drifters crowded the herring dock patiently facing the long wait. Their crews returned to the farms, to other country jobs or employment in the town. Some became smacksmen.

A fresh herring gave us an enjoyable meal very tasty and satisfying. At a penny for a succulent big one and two smaller ones for the same money, it was welcomed by hard pressed local families.

We enjoyed them too especially when cooked mother's way called "snautching", from the deep crosscuts to the bone on both sides. She coated them liberally with flour and fried them vigorously until the skin turned a beautiful crispy brown. "Snautching" quickly ensured cooking right to the bone, it also helped to deny the complaint of those who refused them "because of all those bones".

them in the large rectangular area behind the trawl market separating it from the herring market. I had to clamber down a heavily timbered wall, about three feet, to get to it. Immediately behind the wall were some railway lines, trucks and large, box like vans. Here were the horses, their job to haul those great loads, filled or empty. They were magnificent both in appearance and action. Large, well fed and beautifully groomed. Also well trained and treated, as I could see by the reactions between them, and their handler in the regulation Great Eastern uniform, with it's peaked cap.

Sunday Market – the church has gone!

Sometimes she soused them, a kind of pickling which turned the skin greyish, and the flesh almost colourless. Father liked them – we didn't. At the end of one season Uncle Bob persuaded mother to buy a box of red herrings. They had an attractively coloured bronzey and reddish skin and their flesh a dark brown, stringy and tough and very salty. All these came from their curing which included a lengthy stay in brine. Nobody liked them much – too salty and not tasty enough.

Of my many memories of the market, one persists clearly – possibly it seems at first out of context – the Great Eastern Railway horses. I discovered

He yoked a pair to a large, loaded truck using heavy chains, I saw them haul three empty vans. A quiet word from the handler brought an exciting explosion of power. They threw themselves against the braces – enthusiastically to my eyes. Their hind hooves, pointing downwards. Steel upon stone brought a shower of sparks. Head downward, necks arched, taut muscles. Sometimes the wheels turned at the first pull. At times they had to try again and again. No whip, no shouting, perhaps just a pull on the reins. As the wheels moved more readily they relaxed until the truck seemed to move by itself. At times, as if with relief and enthusiasm, they broke into a trot. I saw a very young horse attempt a gallop! The handler very quickly brought him to order.

In my earlier days just horse drawn vans and carts came. They delivered or took away a host of things, fishing gear, sails, ropes, boxes of fish, barrels of herrings, salt, ice.

My older brother Victor helped in the daily delivery of the last, absolutely essential for the stowing of the fish and it's arrival on the market as fresh as possible.

By the time I went with Victor the smacksmen no longer relied upon

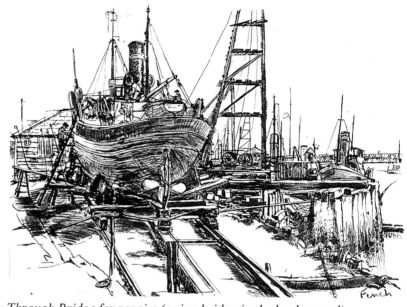

Through Bridge for repairs (swing bridge in the background)

The day after Boxing Day – the owner's there, only a hurricane could keep them in harbour!

Mother Nature for ice – they even had imported it – there was now on the way to Oulton Broad an ice factory. Without understanding how they did it, I enjoyed my frequent visits, especially the final stages. With a sudden whirr the complicated machinery, half seen in the gloom at the back of the echoing interior, sprang to life. Part of it moved forwards and then large, slender, rectangular,

know it was a school day because I played truant intrigued by the rumours. The weather was so much in keeping with the sad sight of the unkempt Belgian fishing craft – always so much less trim than ours. Even the ships as they approached the quay side looked sad to me. Their decks were crowded with Belgian refugees brutally forced to flee their homes and country by the Germans. Men,

Waiting at the shipyard (original exhibited at the Royal Academy)

slightly tapering blocks of ice glided free and moved in my direction. Some were loaded, using large scissor like grips, upon Victor's cart and off we went to that space behind the trawl market. Here it was crushed and delivered to the smack in the state I saw as it was shot from baskets to "below" on Crimson Rose.

My most poignant memory of the market goes back to a grey rather blustery day in 1915. I do

women, children, fathers, mothers, grandfathers, grandmothers, big children, small children, tiny toddlers, babies in arms packed tightly on the narrow decks. Their physical sufferings on the voyage I could plainly see, their mental agony was beyond me. Clothing untidy, faces grimy, men unshaven, women pale and drawn, the children alone showed some animation in marked contrast. As they filed like cattle on to the quayside I saw

The Inner Harbour

pathetic bundles, snatched together and tied in panic. Suitcases crammed, some beyond bursting. A child or two clasped a doll or a teddy.

Their silence was too intense. On the quayside I was reminded of sheep herded into a corner, scared, puzzled, worried and ready at any moment to panic. Helpers moved quickly amongst them. Some were taken home by sympathetic volunteers.

The Lowestoft of my childhood was a world in almost total isolation, particularly to a child. I used to be awake at night unsuccessfully trying to visualise "beyond my town". I always finished with the same picture beginning with my home, our road, our school and spreading to the market, the harbour, shops, and so on, all familiar things, totally enclosed by a high wooden fence; beyond it, nothing – A lot of grown ups seemed to have the same picture! So it is understandable that the landing of just one particular fish was "newsworthy" enough to hurry the local reporter accompanied by the photographer to the market. Sufficient also for

the leading local fishmonger quickly to buy and display it in his window.

It was a sturgeon. The first landed for several years. I went to see it in the fishmonger's window. It was easily the biggest fish I had ever seen.

I have learned since that the sturgeons, so very rarely caught in the North Sea, are usually five to six feet long and can reach twelve feet.

"Sturgeons", Aunt Sarah said, "belong to the King and should always be sent to him". For a time I pondered over what she also said, "Sturgeon is partly meat and chicken as well as fish". I studied this one, especially at the cuts. They all looked the same to me. Perhaps she meant the taste!

There was the Sunday Market, quiet, echoing and clean. Empty, too, except for the occasional strollers. No crews on board waiting for skipper. No skippers boarding the smacks expecting to say very soon "We'll go". Everything waited until the outburst of Monday morning. No smack went to sea. If one arrived she snuggled quickly down, and her crew hurried home to make the best of precious extra hours of freedom.

There was also the afternoon to evening market – just as empty and quiet. Clean too, those men in heavy boots, protected by waterproof aprons and wielding hoses and large brooms, had worked miracles. They also seemed to have banished the smell of fish.

The Christmas Market was in a way a repetition of the other two – with marked differences. The most apparent was the forest of masts as skippers so packed in their smacks that it seemed impossible easily to unpack on the early morning of the day after Boxing Day with the outburst of normal market and it's hectic life. Skippers vied for water, ice, coal, food to get away. Only a hurricane could stop them – or hold them back for a while. The owner was there! Each waited impatiently for the opportunity to free his ship from the tangle of smacks in the harbour. Father said, that once he left in the late afternoon!

Those were the markets when we boys clambered from smack to smack, climbed the rigging and swung from any available rope. We gave Feet and Six Striker – those ever ready market bobbies – a busy time.

When we spoke of the market, that included the harbour. To most people they were inseperable. So if father said, "I'm going to the market", that could also mean "to the harbour", or even, "to the smack".

Lowestoft had three harbours, the trawl dock, the herring dock and the inner harbour approached through the open swing bridge. This was where they went to the slipway, the dry dock and the ship yards for "a goin' over". Here there was also a fascinating variety of ships large and small, some steamers and some under sail. Frequently there were foreigners.

I wandered freely. I asked questions. I sketched. How pleased I am that I still have drawings of an inner harbour which has gone. Nobody interfered. When father was there "in dock", "on the slip", or "in the dry dock", so was I, offering to help as well as sketching.

Today, as with the market, unfortunately banned for school children, the interested local adults and visitors, "You need a permit!"

Chapter 11

Religious?

It must have been Grandfather Finch's house, The Fisherman's Bethel and Grandfather Macey's regular Sunday morning hymn singing that prompted my question to an old smacksman resting in the Fishermen's Shelter, which used to stand at the entrance to the Lowestoft Yacht Basin. "Would you say that fishermen are religious?" He thought for a moment. "Oi don't roitly know", he said, "but they've got the' fear a God in 'm".

It seemed to me that when they "got religion" they got it badly as an elderly cook inferred. He sailed with one. "'E fairly got us scared with it". So scared that "'e got us all t' pray!"

I am still grateful to Aunt Sarah for taking me to the Fisherman's Bethel. I have looked up "bethel" in the dictionary. It says, "a hallowed spot" and "a seaman's church – ashore or floating". Both fit the Lowestoft Fisherman's Bethel with it's almost violent outpouring of belief with no frills.

I heard a similar religious outpouring on a quiet summer evening in Aunt Sarah's back garden when she said, "Can you hear that?" I heard a distant voice loud and clear, but no words. This was no ordinary voice telling of ordinary everyday things. "That's old So and So", Aunt Sarah said (what a pity I have forgotten his name). "He's an old fisherman. He often preaches on Sundays on the beach". He was at least two miles away.

I don't think Grandfather Macey had "got religion badly". He did not go to church or speak of God or Jesus. Yet his kindliness, the overall impact of his voice and his personality were always so pleasing and, as it were, right. He was so warmly welcomed by all of us. I was not surprised by what I saw and heard when I visited him many times when he was very ill. Every Sunday morning, against all advice from his doctor and pleadings from Granny, he scrambled from his bed to his creaking wicker armchair by the window. He held his rather crumpled hymn sheet. With the nodding of his head, the legacy from his accident at sea, emphasised by the brightness of the window behind, he sang through his complete repertoire. He had a pleasing, light baritone voice. I remember poignantly as he sang his favourite hymn, "Rock of Ages", with increasing quivering of his hands and nodding of his head.

When I stayed with Granny Finch there was no need for anybody to tell me that Grandfather had "got religion badly".

I never knew him. He was drowned at sea the year I was born, but he was very much alive throughout the house. Even his freemason's certificate, beautifully framed, dominated the front room, the one reserved for high days and holidays, weddings and funerals. The eye glaring from the centre of the certificate I thought was God's, angry with me because I was naughty. I knew I deserved it because I had done so many of the naughty things, embroidered clearly on Grandfather's samplers which hung on the walls each side of me as I approached the front room.

Going to bed at Granny Finch's was a kind of sermon. Halfway up the stairs on the left hand wall hung a large black and white picture in a dark frame. It puzzled me. Why should a lady with lovely, long dark hair choose to wear a long white nightdress, to sit on a rock, so that she could fling her arms around a great big stone cross which reached well above her head, in the middle of a raging storm with great, frightening waves rushing at her? It was called "Rock of Ages".

On the landing at the top of the stairs stood a large music box, beautifully encased in shining wood. It played lovely tunes – all hymns.

Snuggled down in bed the last thing I saw before falling asleep, and the first on waking up, was a companion picture. It was the same size and framed with the same kind of dark wood as the other. Like the other, it puzzled me. It showed the same lady, in the same night dress. Now she had large wings and looked happier, but, a little bit worried. As well she might. Because, there was a silly little girl with long, very tidy ringlet curls, dressed in a party frock and shoes – chasing a butterfly! Why did she choose to go all by herself along a narrow, twisting rocky path, with an almost vertical rocky mountain on one side and on the other a steep drop to an ugly rock and cavity strewn valley hundreds of feet down? I noticed that the lady stretched a protective hand towards the girl. This one was called "The Guardian Angel".

Did Grandfather's religion pass to his dog "Spot"? So named because of a dark splodge around one eye. On the evidence of a somewhat irate Salvation Army officer it could have come to pass.

He called late one Sunday afternoon. Grandfather answered the door. There stood the officer. "Do you own a white rough coated dog with a black mark around one eye?" Grandfather admitted to ownership. "Please could you keep him in on

Sunday afternoons? He completely spoils our service". My doubtless nonplussed Grandfather said he would do so. The full story went something like this.

A high ranking Salvation Army officer lived in a nearby road. Each Sunday afternoon a group, headed by a band marched towards his house. With them marched a white, rough coated dog with a dark patch around one eye. Outside that special house they formed a circle and in that circle stood that same small white dog. The band struck up. The people joined in. So did the small dog. He moved into the centre by the side of the officer, probably to increase the effectiveness of his contribution.

I can clearly visualise myself sitting on the edge of Granny Finch's horse hair sofa, the backs of my knees becoming increasingly painful, for a long time in silence, because she strictly enforced the rule "little boys should be seen and not heard".

On the facing wall hung two framed photographs; one of Grandfather wearing the fisherman's peaked cap of his day; the other of Uncle Teddy in his Eton collar and Norfolk jacket, lost with his father in the same terrible accident at sea. As they stared down at me, and I back at them, they seemed to come alive. The muzziness around them, resulting from the vignetted portrait convention of the time, turned into clouds – they've already got to heaven!

Religion was much in the air, even in the Town Hall. There were strictly observed regulations for Sundays, Christmas Day and Easter Day.

No shops open – except for tobacco, sweets and newspapers, and they closed at midday. Trams stopped earlier. The street lights dimmed earlier. The "pitchers" (picture houses) closed, no football, the beach empty except for one or two religious gatherings. Whether there was a town council ruling on the last I do not know, but, something was strictly observed. Perhaps it was partly because the boys wore their Sunday best, and the girls their dainty Sunday frocks. There was quite a stir when the Town Hall granted a licence for a cinema to open at Easter.

The market was silent except for an occasional fisherman or two "rolling" along and chatting – about ships and fish probably. Smacks arrived. None went to sea. I frequently tried to persuade father "to work it" so that he arrived on Saturday. We could go to a football match in the afternoon and have him all day Sunday.

Not only was there a strong religious lobby in the Town Hall but Lowestoft had more than it's fair share of churches and chapels – and a Salvation Army citadel and a Band of Hope. Even the Mormons showed up! The smack, cum-chapel–cum–medical centre, belonging to The Mission to Deep Sea Fishermen, was a frequent visitor to the harbour. I could easily pick her out. She was always so neat and tidy. She had white sails instead of the rich tan of all the other work–a–day smacks. She had the registration letters L.O. for London instead of the L.T. for Lowestoft – and – her skipper had a smart uniform, with a shiny peaked cap and a dog–collar.

Religion was very much in the air of the schools. I was reminded of it's sway from way back in father's school days, when he picked up a john dory and spoke of Jesus feeding the five thousand. When I went to school many years later it was still there and very much alive. We had a morning assembly with hymns and The Lord's Prayer just as he had. We had daily scripture lessons and we memorised passages as he had. We ended morning school and began the afternoon with a sung grace. We ended the day, again with a sung grace. The schools closed on Thursday afternoon throughout the summer otherwise they would be almost empty of children enjoying their Sunday School outing.

Every evening that father was home he saw our going to bed ceremony – unfortunately he never took part. Mother on a chair. We, in strict order of seniority, lined up. Victor, the oldest moved first. He knelt by mother's knee. His head in her lap. She often stroked his hair. In a clear voice he said The Lord's Prayer followed by the family "made up" one. This always began, "God bless mummy and daddy, all my brothers and sisters". From here he could spread his blessings to a favourite relative, a favourite friend, the dog, the cat. The younger ones never forgot a doll or a teddy. This prayer must end with the plea "and please God make me a good boy (or girl)". Rene followed Victor and the recognised format. Next came my turn. I can still feel the warmth and safety of her lap and the satisfying pressure of her hands upon my head. On and on we went. Never a hint of boredom.

One effect of our going to bed ceremony, helped by my Sunday School attendances, infrequent until Christmas and the summer outing neared, I became a church–chapel wanderer. Every Sunday I went, quite haphazardly, and with no hint from a grown up, to a church or a chapel or the Salvation Army, and for no reason that I can recall, never to the Roman Catholics. I think they were not popular in historically puritan Suffolk. The Mormons issuing from a small, highly varnished door not far from the Public Library, all dressed in long black overcoats and broad brimmed trilbies, their faces very stern, scared me.

Black Widders!

God", I later reported to mother. She didn't laugh or smile. "What was He like", she said. I told her, "He was like an old fisherman with the usual white ruffle beard around his chin .... and he wore a sou'wester". I described the huge open book with it's pages divided into squares. "It had my name on it", I told her. "I thought he was sad because so many of my squares were shaded black because of my naughtiness". She smiled now. "Whose fault is that?", she said.

The attitude of fishermen towards clergymen and even nuns appears to me, now, as a mixture of age old superstitions, perhaps tinged with suspicion. Even father who usually dismissed such fanciful ideas did not exactly like it when mother allowed the local visiting curate to have bed and breakfast at our house once a month, when we were living in Cornwall.

Another result, helped by mother's frequent references to the Almighty when I was naughty, "God won't like that", at times she did substitute Grandfather Macey! So, it turned out on a lovely summer morning as I lay on my back enjoying the beautiful white massed clouds, "I'm sure I saw

I can recall three stories of smacksmen and people of the cloth.

The mate had everything ready on board. Skipper arrived. He reappeared on deck in his sea clothes. He spoke with his mate. "Let's go", he said. He glanced up to the top of the quay. There stood a

"Oim not a goin, take 'er inter th' trawl dock!"

"You whiskered old So and So – If you want poor fishermen to starve why not let 'em starve at home"

clergyman, clearly absorbed in the activity on board his smack. "Pack up!" he ordered sharply, "We a not a goin' this morn'n!"

The next story is somewhat bizarre. I must first explain the setting. This smack had "gone thru' bridge" some days earlier for "a goin' over". This meant being taken by a tug into the inner harbour where lay the dry dock and slip–way, both necessary for work on the under water parts of a ship. To allow them to pass from the outer to the inner docks, the bridge linking North and South parts of the town was opened. Pedestrians and all traffic were halted and to prevent accidents a barrier was placed on each side of the gap. Quickly traffic and pedestrians piled up. The smack approached hauled by a tug – a paddle steamer designed for the job. It passed through on it's way to sea. Skipper looked up at people waiting by the barriers. He saw two nuns! "Black widders" they called them. "Go in t' th' trawl dock!", he shouted to the tug captain, "Oi've changed me moind". The astounded tugman had to turn sharply, and dangerously, to port.

The third story brings variety – and a touch of doubt! – because it introduces a clergyman who frequently roamed the market and spoke to all and sundry. He chatted to the men as they worked on board. No skipper refused to go to sea because he "overlooked" his ship! He even went for a trip on a herring drifter. I came to know him because he frequently passed me on his way to the Church of St Margaret or to his house. He was Vicar of Lowestoft. I can still see him waving cheerily from his old bicycle, a tall spare figure often in a flowing black cloak which on a breezy day threatened to tangle with the spokes of the rear wheel. During the herring season one or two herrings dangled from the handle bars.

God, religious lessons at school or superstition I do not know which – perhaps a mixture of them all – surfaced at odd times.

This one came from father – exploding into a furious temper – for the only time in his life I'm almost sure, and justifiably as I hope to prove.

The weather is tantalisingly fitful. A steady trawling wind, trawl shot. In a half an hour or so it drops away to a calm. Up comes the trawl. Down below go the crew. Later, up springs a good trawling wind. Up comes the crew. Down goes the trawl. Down below goes the crew. The smack bowls along busily. On this day such a sequence dragged through too frequently for father.

He hurried to the bow, arms flung in the air, fists clenched, face turned skywards –"You whiskered old So and So", he shouted. " If you want poor fishermen to starve! Why not let'm starve at home!"

Perhaps a tinge of all three came into the accepted attitude towards seagulls. I heard of fishermen who believed the souls of their work mates passed immediately at death into a gull. So, that rear guard gull who gazed down so intently and mewed so softly as he repeatedly swept from stem to stem – was, "Ole Charlie O doid last week", perhaps.

I never saw or heard of cruelty to or the shooting of a gull. We boys playing on the stony part of the beach aimed at tin cans, at any floating object – at one another! – but never at a seagull.

I am pretty sure that father, possibly because of our "going to the prayers" at mother's knee, of echoes of distant school lessons, and, for at least twenty years, the influence of his "bible thumping" father, was mindful of God.

When during my teens, we spoke of such things, "I don't rightly know", he said, a typical smacksman's verbal side step. He then spoke of "Davey Jones", who, "Always wins in the end" – a blend of God and Father Neptune! He would always win if father, the seaman, allowed him. Inevitably there would come the time when he had to retire from the battle but Davey would continue on his way.

Was there in this a hint of the fatalism which I also found when talking about safety and survival?

I am sure that once at sea, even on my first trip, fear never touched me. Neither did I sense it from the men – and the North Sea can be treacherous even in summer time. Mother, who knew of the dangers, never said, "Do take care", and, "Don't do this or that", as I left for my trips. Perhaps she impressed these upon father in private. He spoke of many things on our walk to the harbour, but not of her fears, nor of his own.

I became so confident on my first trip that I persuaded Decky to rig me a swing – and got him into trouble and myself a severe telling off. I shudder now as I see myself swinging way over the sea and looking down at the waves only too ready to receive me. Father came. He spoke a few words to Decky which turned his face very red. He was as angry with me as ever before or since.

The taller the waves I faced from my favourite place, way up in the bows, the more I enjoyed them.

I was afraid – once. Not for myself but for father as I watched him on that climb to the very top of the main top mast wearing his heavy thigh boots.

Alfie, my infant school friend told his mother that I swore at my mother. On our way to school he had put to me a rhetorical question. "You swear at your mother, don't you?" I can only think that bravado in a boy of seven to live up to "the bigness" implicit in the question made me say, "Yes", which was a black lie and I knew it. The next morning I called for Alfie. His mother answered the door, "Alfie isn't coming to school with you anymore", she said, "We don't like little boys who swear at their mummy" and she shut the door. A day or so later my mother said angrily, "You are a very naughty boy. You know you don't swear at me. Nobody swears in our house!" It appeared that Alfie's father, who sailed on the same smack with my father, had complained to him, and, he had told mother. "Daddy told him the truth", she said. "Now you must go to Alfie's house and say you are sorry". His father opened the door. "What a silly boy you are", he said. "Your father has put me right". Alfie and I went to school together.

Were they fatalists? I'm sure there is a strong hint in father's overall reaction to his owner's decision in 1916, at the height of the attacks on our smacks, "It'll be better if you take Crimson Rose to Padstow". Better, because free from the German submarines and mines which infested his usual fishing grounds – but what about the dangers of the sailing to the west'd? Mines and submarines through the entire voyage even into the Atlantic. He did it in a sailing smack built for the North Sea. His crew either older or younger men because of the "call up" for the Navy. His reply agreeing to the owner's strongly implied order, must have been coloured in his mind by "There it is. I've got to go. I'll do the best I can – if not ..."

A hint of fatalism came from Skipper Frank Martins voice and attitude when he left our home to rejoin the Atlantic convoys after his two ships had been destroyed by German torpedoes.

Was it fatalism which made Bob Barley visit us to say good-bye the very first time he had called in on his way back to his ship and to his last trip?

A strong hint of it came from their comments on survival, undoubtedly from the fact that if anything went seriously wrong it was "up t' us". In their isolated life they knew that the hope of rescue or help of any kind was minimal. This emerged clearly as we spoke about swimming and I learned that so few of them could swim. Father was one. "I haven't bothered", he said. Others said, "Oid rather go quickly". Another said, "If Oi could swim Oi could 'ang on f'r a bit. Oi'd 'ave t' give up in the end", and another, "Woiy 'ang it out".

Grandfather Macey was a powerful swimmer. He kept himself afloat until rescued although semi–conscious and with a crushed forehead and a smashed arm. Young Owen Martin, another strong swimmer, drowned in a few minutes in full view of his brother, also a powerful swimmer, but restrained by father, who explained to the Coroner, "I didn't want to lose two men", and, "the sea was running too high". Father went overboard once, but there was somebody near enough to drag him back.

At the inquest on Owen the Coroner asked, "Why didn't you throw the lifebelt?" Father replied, "I dared not. It's so heavy I couldn't aim it properly, and I was afraid of hitting him". The Coroner could not have known much about a smack's life belt – "Throw it!" I tried. I could just lift it from it's socket at the back of the companion way. Father speaking of one of their most important and most ready to hand safety equipment, and complain of it's weight!

The little boat – the smack's life boat – was truly cumbersome, extremely heavy and impossible to launch quickly. Grandfather in his agony must have endured many minutes whilst they cleared it's clutter, dragged and lifted it up and to the rail, dropped it overboard and finally reached him. Yet every little boat I saw was cluttered. Not one smack had davits to speed the launching. I neither saw nor heard of life–boat drill, nor did I discover any survival kit when they did get afloat.

This attitude spread to the owners. They, and even the insurance people, did nothing about it. So far as I am aware neither did the men.

I found father's life jacket in the bottom of his bunk – and under piles of bedding, clothing and newspapers. It was a clumsy collection of heavy, thinnish cork slabs, in a thick, white canvas kind of waistcoat, with long fastening tapes at the back. "Do you practice using this?", I said. "No", he said, "it's too much bother".

I discovered a rocket in the junk cupboard of East Dean. If there were any on other smacks I never heard of or came across one.

They were most punctilious over the rigging of their smack. "Look after that", father said, "and she'll never let you down". Also Cooky always took great care of the port and starboard, and, of the mast head and the fishing lights. Their casing always sparkled brilliantly and never a smudge on the glass. He always put t hem in position at the correct time e very evening. Thus father and Cooky minimised the danger of things going wrong!

I have not answered, "Were they religious?" I don't think I can, but, I can say that they were aware of God and that they sensed him in their work and in their weather. They spoke of him in whatever terms and by whatever name came to mind. I recall the story told to me by a retired Lowestoft master shipwright I have mentioned earlier.

It begins when he was ten, the age at which his smacksman father thought he might follow him later. He was not very keen. They agreed on three trial trips. Two passed. At the end of the second, "I wasn't quite sure". The third made his mind up for him. "We ran into the worst storm for years", he said. "Father wouldn't allow me on deck". They were tightly battened down as the storm grew. His father did allow him one quick peep. "I saw two drenched men fighting the tiller and the deck awash". As the storm intensified he witnessed something which he could never forget. "I saw strong men on their knees praying".

Chapter 12

Characters

All smacksmen were out of the ordinary and so "a bit of a character", and a goodly number, "real characters". This was certainly true of all my smacksmen. Some were "real characters" who exuded, "Oim what Oi am. Take't or leave't".

Skipper Chambers was certainly one. We, my wife and I, met him at his terraced cottage. We noticed that he had joined with the other householders in an overall, very tasteful colour scheme, for the outside of their terraced homes, which made their street most attractive. No shrinking shyness from Skipper. This was most marked when I introduced my wife, whom he treated with "old world" courtesy and to whom he chatted about himself and more about his home. It was neatness and orderliness itself. He took her to "'ave a look" but, he insisted, without me, "'e wouldn't cott'n on". Our general conversation was by no means restricted to himself and his home. I remember too his apology to my wife for using the word "damn" in the telling a story, "I had to", he said, "so I could tell the yarn properly!"

Later he wrote me a letter. It's clarity, grammar, spelling and the hand writing, after a gap of some fifty years, proved how well they taught at school which he left when he was twelve.

He illustrated it with a delightful pen drawing of a smack in full sail with it's number LT363 on the mains'l – obviously one he skippered. In the distance, lightly drawn – and in correct perspective – is another smack. to the right of LT363 is a steep cliff – very like the one a short walk from his house – on it a tree and a lighthouse, there are a few gulls. He added a title – "Happy Days"!

Skipper Reeve, another of them, wrote in 1972 of the toughness of life on a smack and especially as Cooky at the age of fourteen with his father as Skipper. His summing up could not be bettered by a leader writer in "The Times": -

"When I look at trawling now and what we used to go through in the old smacks it makes me wonder how we survived. They were wooden ships and iron men in those days. Now they're Iron ships and wooden men".

I have unfortunately forgotten the name of the one who thus succinctly and brilliantly summarised the human aspect of fishing on a smack, "When you left the pier heads all friendships ceased".

Skipper Chambers writes – and draws

We were greeted by Skipper Orso Osborne and his wife in their most attractive caravan set among others in a landscaped park. We met with the same courtesy and interesting conversation. He insisted we called him Orso. The attractive appearance of their home, we learned, was due to him. "Moi wife c'n do very little", he said, "Oi 'ave t' do most 've th' cook'n as well". She was almost crippled with arthritis. Both insisted that we stayed for coffee and that we must accept momentoes of our visit. They took these from the sideboard, "Shan't want these for too long". He had a remarkable memory for names and registration numbers of the smacks. "None a me pals c'n trip me up", he claimed. "His pals", mostly retired seamen, met by Oulton Broad each morning. "Troi me wi' one", he said. I tried him with two or three – no hesitation with the right answers.

Another personality springs to mind – Mr Wales who lived a few doors from us. We all, even father, spoke of him as Mister.

There was something which made us treat him with respect. Perhaps it was his courteous manner, his direct, crisply delivered conversation. Possibly it was his appearance, his neatness of dress, or that crisply white perfectly adjusted collar and carefully fashioned tie. Perhaps, even more so, it was his eager face, directly gazing eyes. Then there were those cheeks, always looking as if polished by a scrubbing with very hot water and carbolic soap. His reply to my question completes the picture.

I wanted to draw, correctly, smacks with their sails set to suit the wind. His reply included hints of calculus and trigonometry which I was then studying. He also had attended a Board School, his higher mathematics came from experience and understanding of the behaviour of sails.

Skipper Frank Martin, hero of my early days, was not at all impressive on shore and, unlike many of the others, on retirement he could scarcely be rated as a character. My final memory comes from the last time I met him. His second wife stood by and Skipper Frank clung to her arm as if he had already accepted old age. Sadly I recalled the

Skipper Frank

outstanding and confident Skipper, his amazing strength and as a powerful swimmer. I recalled how as father said, "He is careful with his money", which enabled him to buy his own house and to order, from Brixham his home town, and pay for, the tosher "Crecy". I remember how he and father, just the two of them, sailed and worked Crecy throughout the whole of one summer.

What a contrast with Larko Lark, like the tough swashbuckler he was, remains the nearest to a fictional seaman I ever met – but without the raucous voice and the "'Eave to! Me 'arties".

As a "lucky Skipper" – one who consistently landed profitable catches – he prospered longer than most, but, his liking for a jug or two brought him warnings from The Owner. Finally he was Called to The Office.

This is my account of that interview based upon father's story.

Larko went in, cap on head, I am sure it stayed there. He faced The Owner seated at his desk.

The Owner, "I see, Mr. Lark, your returns have not been so good for quite a while" – Larko, no reply. The Owner, "I've been thinking – I reckon it's about time you had a bit of a rest". Larko, no noticeable reaction. The Owner,"So, Mr. Lark, I've decided to send Mr.——— as Skipper on East Dean for a week or two!" Immediately from Larko, "Loike 'ell y'do. She's moiy ship 'n no other bugger's a goin' t' take 'er out!". He probably gave The Owner's desk a mighty bang at the same time. He stormed out.

An hour or so later East Dean left harbour. At her tiller stood Larko. Whether it was the aftermath of that interview or not, from that trip on, Larko quickly became once more "A Lucky Skipper" – and a more careful drinker.

The moral of the next Larko story is that a skipper who "loikes 'is point" should take care.

Father was up forrard as East Dean, with Larko at the tiller, approached the two pier heads forming the harbour mouth. She lurched slightly. With his mind concentrating on the moving of the bowsprit he took little notice. She lurched again and now was heading for the south pier only a few yards ahead. He looked back at the tiller – No skipper! No time to search! He raced aft and steered East Dean safely by the massive pier timbers. "We may have scraped them a bit", he said. No sign of skipper on deck. Had he gone overboard? Father hurried below. There was skipper! – squatting by the opened galley fire, shovel in hand, frying a bloater. "He was lucky", father said. "He would have lost his ticket if anybody in authority had seen what happened".

I once experienced a very different Larko, when I needed him! We had just left harbour. I could see Lowestoft clearly astern. I settled on a narrow ledge by the ship's rail and a few feet from Decky now on watch.

As usual the weather seemed duller and cooler beyond the pier heads and, as usual, I doubted the wisdom of my coming. This I knew always passed quickly. Decky whistled quietly. He moved the tiller sharply. A wave must have risen behind me – a large one by the weight of icy water which fell on my head and cascaded green and cold over every inch of my body and every stitch of my clothing. I sat immobile lost in drenched icey misery. Then I heard Larko's voice unusually quiet and soothing. I was in no state even to begin to appreciate the contrast. "Come a long a me", it said, "Oi've got just the thing f'yer". He hastened and half carried me to the welcome warmth of the fug down below and near to the great boiler. He hurried me from my dripping clothes and boots. He dried me painfully with a large towel as abrasive as horse hair. "Finish orf", he said and handed it to me. He soon returned and rushed me into a garnsey which fell amply to my ankles. He enveloped my legs in thick boot

stockings which trailed feet beyond my toes. He left me again. He came back with Cooky's baking tin. "'Ere y'are", he said, "Get this down yer". I looked quickly at the greasy contents, some anonymous bits swilled about in it. My stomach moved – but I managed to "down" more than I thought possible at first sight. Nicer than I feared despite a taste new to me. "Probably brandy", father decided later.

The new ministering angel Larko had not yet finished. He helped me into the cabin. He pointed to a bed of clothing and a blanket on the floor under the table. "Git y'ead down there", he said. I obeyed and immediately fell asleep.

I awoke completely recovered – Larko's "sommat" certainly had something! I went straight to father, wary of smacksman's humour. "Do you think that Decky played a trick on me?" I asked. "No", he answered after a lengthy pause, "I don't think so – that kind of thing can happen at anytime". He wasn't convincing – I still think Decky wiggled the tiller at "the right time".

I must include three other characters, two lived in the same row of terraced houses in Lowestoft as ourselves. The one immediately next door, Skipper Keeble, I remember because of the superiority which he and his household assumed in my imagination, simply because he was Skipper of one of the very few Lowestoft steam trawlers. They earned "bigger money" than a sailing smack!

Next door on the other side lived a retired fisherman whose name I have forgotten, but, I do remember him as a gentle, kindly old man who sold ice–cream. This he made and sold in a shed in his back garden to eke out his very sparse income – no "hand outs" in those days – one penny for a generous wafer, a half–penny for a piled up cornet. I can see him so clearly pulling back the damp sacking cover of the tin container and ladling out the lovely ice–cream. I am afraid that he contravened most hygiene regulations, particularly of today – nobody complained!

The third lived several doors away – Skipper Woolnough, highly successful and respected. "I'm expecting him in today", his wife said as she told me to sit down in her spotless kitchen warmed by the blazing fire of her massive, highly polished cooking range. "He likes a bit of warmth", she said, and positioned his chair near the fire. "He likes his paper too" and she placed the Lowestoft Journal nearby on the massive kitchen table. Skipper arrived. He slipped off his jacket and his heavy boots and settled back in his chair. Mrs. Woolnough picked up the paper. She sat down. She began to read aloud. Skipper couldn't.

One old man told me, "Oi 'ad seven brothers. All on'em skippers – but only one could read or write".

I must not forget Skipper "Stumpy" James. "Stumpy" suited him so well – a good example of the fishermen's apt choice of a nickname. He was stumpy in build and stumped along as he walked. He lived nearby. His two boys were close friends of my brother Frank. "Stumpy" in a way suited his personality. Whenever I met him he always had a breezy greeting which "stumped" out.

He probably stumped at the U–boat officer soon to torpedo his smack, who said he liked us and our country. "Why th' 'ell d' y want t' sink my ship for". As a teenager he sailed on Atlantic windjammers. He became Skipper of the Board of Fisheries research ship, The George Bligh, a very prestigious job. He remained the same old "Stumpy".

There are three others who return as clearly – but – I can only remember them as Cooky and two Deckies. Skipper and the others often used their Christian names but never surnames. So to me they had to be addressed by their job – in those days a boy – or a teenager – always addressed a grown up as Mrs. or Mr. or by their job.

My first Decky I sailed with on Crimson Rose. He was probably sixteen or seventeen and to me a grown up man. His "book larn'n" had ended at either twelve or fourteen. He showed an enviable mastery of his job. The reactions of Skipper Frank Martin, the most demanding of them all, underlined this. I liked him because he treated me more like a grown up. He had a great sense of fun. He was a great tease. This I discovered as he faced me when I first used the tub. He played beautifully the young smacksman's musical instrument, the mouth organ, long before the days of Larry Adler when it became the harmonica. His playing on a quiet evening at sea is unforgettable. He had many tunes. How he learned them is a mystery. His 75 pence a week (just over 15p), and "'elp'n out at 'ome", did not allow the cost of the still rare gramophone. This left the pub and the old man who, on Saturday nights, sold penny song sheets, words only.

He must have been among the earliest of the Lowestoft cinema buffs. We had two cinemas – "the pitchers" – a penny (less than $\frac{1}{2}$p) or tuppence a time, rising to sixpence. I soon learned he was a "Red Injun" fan – I was too. So we swopped stories. These led to a game in which I was the white and he the red man. He was to creep up on myself, seated on the cabin top, gazing into the vastness of the prairie. He stealthily advanced

tomahawk – his razor sharp shet knife – open at the ready.

Unexpectedly Crimson Rose almost as if she wanted to add a touch of realism, lurched violently. Decky stumbled forward. His shet knife plunged into my left knee. I still have the scar. What happened next I cannot remember.

I recall Decky of East Dean as a more robust character, about the same age as the other and "a bit 'f a show off", who boasted, "Oi reck'n Oi c'n 'oist th' mizz'n 'n swear all a th' toime withou' repeat'n m'self".

I was very sorry for him and critical of Skipper Larko, after he dashed on deck, following the tremendous unexpected squall which all but capsized East Dean.

Cooky, I met several years later on Crimson Rose. He was very different from the two Deckies. He was much older. His face was sunken and pallid, his build spare and – apparently – frail. He had a quiet voice and manner which, became very decisive as I learned, on my first trip with him, when I began to wash my hands under the tap which was only "f' cook'n", and, when I dared to enter the cabin near the end of the voyage when he was "a doin'" his "toidy'n up". It still surprises me that he withstood the toughness of his several jobs.

How did he control the mighty warp, especially at hauling as it came down to him dripping muddy water and slimy seaweed? Also during shooting when hard, dry and abrasive it raced and coiled up and away from him. Such was the job which, a much younger man said, knocked him over and even flung him up and on to the deck.

As far as I could judge he carried out each of his several jobs very well – I ate with relish everything he cooked. They all did. His many mugs of tea satisfied every man on board. The mast head, the starboard and port and the other lights stayed unblemished and always placed at the right time in the right place. He was so successful with the boiler fire that the capstan never faltered because of falling steam pressure.

As for his regular end of trip "toidy'n up", it satisfied Skipper. It would have satisfied his wife if he were unwise enough to let her know of his prowess.

He always wore his cap. At the back a few sparse whisps of hair always straggled. When a gust of wind blew it off I saw those few whisps were almost all he had. I spoke of this to father. "It's because of the war", he said, "he was badly gassed".

I also remember this Cooky especially as the only one on board, including father, who showed interest in my drawings.

Father like many other smacksmen became more and more of a character after he retired. I have a wealth of memories to draw upon!

A story from World War Two reveals his readiness to tackle a fresh problem and what at times was called his stubbornness.

He joined Dad's Army. "You're too old", they told him, as if that made any difference! So they gave him a uniform and, month's later, a rifle which he treated as religiously as if it were a compass. In the course of time a Lewis gun arrived. "Anybody know how to handle this thing?" asked the platoon captain. Dead silence. Then, "I'll have a go", said father – a smacksman never refused a challenge. He handled that heavy, cumbersome and lethal weapon like a huge revolver. He shot the target to pieces.

On the following Sunday morning, after tuition from a regular army instructor, father's turn came again, strictly ordered to handle it in the official army way. He missed the target every time. "He never did hit it", the platoon commander said, "if they'd only left him alone, we'd all be sorry for any Germans he met. As it was he became a danger to us!"

Father, despite a strict ban from all the military, decided he must join a battle course with live ammunition. He waited his chance – and went.

"Come back, you silly old bugger!", roared the regular army sergeant. Now, father had put on a bit of weight since retirement which made his nicely rounded backside more or less level with a stream of bullets. At regular intervals mines exploded within a few feet of him. "We can't court martial him", said his commander, "according to our records he doesn't exist!" "I enjoyed myself", he said.

He and mother both enjoyed "the pictures" as they then called the cinema in that very early era of the silent films. Mother preferred the more serious for one simple reason – father's laugh. When Charlie Chaplin, Buster Keaton and the other funny men appeared father's laughter, a kind of explosion, shattered the silence. "People turn round and stare at us", she complained.

I believe that class did not exist for the smacksmen.

I still chuckle as I recall brother Frank's story of father's visit to his Royal Air Force station when he was a humble Aircraftman Class Two. It was so far from the nearest town that, on certain mornings, an ancient coach came to take the shoppers.

Frank and father joined the long queue. It moved slowly forward as soon as the coach arrived and it's door swung open. Immediately in front of them were two ladies clearly of "class" by voice, dress and manner. One of them tripped as she caught her foot on the very high first step. She would have fallen heavily – but for father. He gripped her waist and stood her safely on the top step. "Oopsy! Daisy! dearie", he said. "You must take more water with it next time!" She turned and smiled sweetly, "Indeed I will", she said, "Thank you very much indeed". She was Frank's commanding officer's wife! He didn't know whether to climb on to the roof or under the bus.

Some smacksmen, far too many I learned in later years, were far less fortunate in their retirement than Orso, Skipper Chamber, father and others.

I was about eight when Aunt Sarah took me to visit an aged fisherman relative. I was far too young to grasp the implications of what I was to experience, but, I can recall a vague and persistent feeling of pity, or sorrow perhaps. This stayed with me for the rest of the day and when I went to bed. I overheard her saying to mother before we set out, "He's stuffing it with tobacco". Years later I learned it was cancer in the cheek.

My clearest memory of him is the dressing fastened to a pale, gaunt face by sticking plaster, but despite my staring, I saw no tobacco.

I can clearly see a long, low, dimly lit and bare room. It's scrubbed floorboards are almost concealed by identical iron bedsteads ranked along each side. There is just enough space between them to squeeze in a wooden chair. Sitting on or lying in or standing by their beds are old men. "Their wives have to be in another room", Aunt Sarah said. Standing around or sitting on one of the few wooden chairs are their visitors. Each inmate is wearing an off–white, calico night shirt. Their conversation so low that it scarcely ripples the gloomy silence. "That was the workhouse", mother said, "I can't understand why Aunt Sarah took you there".

I have already spoken of the change in father as we landed on Crimson Rose and how he became the one I knew at home immediately we left her. I have also commented on similar marked changes in Skipper and the crew as they left, they had become the strangers I met on the first day. Skipper Frank Martin on board his ship the impressive, competent master of his job. On a crowded Sunday on the sea front an ordinary smallish man and at our house almost a non-entity who had to be encouraged even to speak. I can remember father as we moved into the crowd at a local football match, greeting an ordinary looking man. "You know who that was",

Father – retired after 50 years of "The Stuff"

I meet the Runners Up

he said to me, "That was Larko!" I had overlooked him.

It would take pages to attempt to give reasons for or explain these changes and probably fail. I will suggest they probably came from attempting consciously or otherwise to adapt to such completely different, perhaps alien, and, to them, a very strange way of life. After all they usually only had to put up with it for a few hours.

I must include Uncle Herbert, father's youngest brother, a shipwright and a man of few words. We were very friendly. He lived nearby and patiently put up with my persistant chatter and questionning about ships and his work. One day he said, "Look at these". He opened a large box. In it were several saws of varying shapes and sizes. He spoke of their special jobs. They were all in beautiful condition. Suddenly he seized one. He placed on his sawing stool a piece of timber about one inch thick. He set to work and without any guide lines and without stopping, he cut a perfect circle. I was about twelve and watched fascinated, as I had already done woodwork at school. As the last cut perfectly met the first, all, I believe, I could say was "Coo!"

To me "the market" included the harbour and the ships. So in my mind I lump the smacksmen with those who worked on the market which teemed with men intent upon one or other of a wide variety of jobs. There were the lumpers who lumped the fish in their clanging metal wheeled trolleys. There were the men who slashed the fish with fearsome knives. There were the market bobbies, and the owners. There were the auctioneers upon whom rested the fortune of the owners and the welfare of their crews.

The two police had little authority beyond the market. If "The Runners Up", my nickname for them, had their way, very little within it. They formed one of the most active, intelligent, resourceful band of twelve year old ruffians it has been my pleasure to meet. As soon as they spotted a smack, one was running away to tell skipper's or the mate's or any crew member's wife that her husband was "a com'n in". For this he received a penny, or "tuppence", or if lucky, "Thrippence".

My one attempt to join them was a complete disaster! Before I realised that tiny dark smudge was a smack one boy shot past me on his way to tell the skipper's wife!

I spoke to an aged long retired "Runner Up". He spoke of their amazing grasp of details by which they recognised a smack. Numbers higher up in the mains'l than the others, one had a long pennant at the mast head, another had a weather vane, yet

94

another had a gold leafed top to it's mainmast. On and on he went. "How did you learn the details about the men", I asked. "We asked a lotta questions", he said.

The Runners Up and the two policemen were made for each other – as natural enemies. One they nicknamed Six Striker – yet another apt choice. "We managed", he said, "t' dodge 'm most 've th' toime – but when that one got me afore I c'd get past 'm 'e give me six a th' best on me arse – 'E wor that quick".

They nicknamed the other "Feet", a very obvious choice for a very obvious reason. "Those great boots", the erstwhile Runner claimed, "took 'm too many toimes t' th' pub". There was one very near to the market.

"Why were they always after you?" I asked. "You ort t' know", he said, "we wore allus there in th' morn'n when we should a bin at school".

The gentle giant

Truanting in those days was a very serious offence, quickly followed by a visit from the attendance officer, a scaring man with a waxed moustache.

He told how the Runners Up defeated a carefully planned alliance between Six Striker and Feet. When Feet – the slower one – was at the end of the jetty where the boys met and from where they had an uninterrupted view to the horizon, Six Striker, very much more agile stationed himself at the other end of the same jetty. They tempted Feet to chase one of them and so draw the attention of Six Striker, who advanced to catch him. As he did so a very fast runner standing nearby dashed behind him and away. "We rather loiked ole Six Striker", he said, "Didn't care much f' Feet".

Long Taylor, "The Gentle Giant" – no need to enlarge upon his nickname! – loomed above everybody. Father, from his five feet seven, spoke to him with his head pressed back as if to somebody in an upstairs window. The Giant's broad brimmed stetson made him more impressive than ever. He had a voice to match! He was a failed owner. "No fault've 'is own", they said. He wasn't tough enough to succeed in that tough world. When one of his smack's was posted missing, he stayed at his office night after night until it returned or was accepted as lost. I often saw him at The Crown Meadow, the home ground of the Lowestoft football club. He was an important member. With him in the annual team photograph the players looked like schoolboys.

"Poor" Sterry clambered from ship to ship and walked around the market selling newspapers. His nickname was only too apt and reflected the sympathy of all who knew him. The market was tough. It could also be just the opposite. Poor Sterry was an epileptic. I can still see him after a serious attack which threw him into the harbour. He lay, seemingly lifeless, on the concrete floor of the market. His clothes oozed it's filthy water. Strands of wet seaweed spread from his dark hair over his pallid face. This picture upset me for a long time.

A mysterious character was "Ole Buck". He looked too old and lethargic for his job. He always rowed his boat standing up. His shoulders hunched. He never seemed to look up and he rarely spoke. He went from smack to smack selling tobacco and sweets. He appeared in the morning. He disappeared round about midday. From whence he came and to where he went, nobody knew.

I can recall only one feminine market character – not surprisingly because of that unwritten law against women. They considered her, "A better

Ole Buck arrives

man th'n 'er father", an owner. Skipper Martin and father sailed for him. She climbed up and down the quayside. She leapt into the rigging and down to the deck as readily as the men. She dressed sensibly. She acted firmly. She knew her job. They reacted to her as if she were indeed a man. Nonetheless it was still strange to me to see a woman on board, and more so, to hear her give orders to skippers. They obeyed her readily too! I have wondered, many times, if she chose the names for her father's smacks. Crimson Rose, Rose of Devon, Heliotrope. Such poetry from her father, whom I knew well, was most unlikely!

The first time I saw him he was talking to Skipper Frank Martin on board Crimson Rose. I thought he was a market hanger on. He certainly did not fit my pre-conceived image of "The Owner". (Some of the men spoke those two word in Capital Letters! After all he held their fortunes in his hands). Then I heard his voice! It changed my opinion. He was the only owner who took his smacks to the harbour mouth.

If any man should be mentioned in capital letters it was The Auctioneer as, in his long white coat, he stepped up from the slime of the market onto his box. His assistant, similarly attired, and wearing his heavy market boots, stood by with note book and a hand bell. This to summon buyers.

I will try to describe the picture of the brief auction which decided the reward of a crew for five or six days hard work.

A crowd gathers around the neatly arranged fish – mostly in rows, and a lot in boxes. Some men stand idly by. Others study the catch. The bell rings. The auctioneer steps onto his box. His assistant opens his note book. The bidding for the first lot begins – and ends quickly. The auctioneer machine guns again in a language as incomprehensible to me as Chinese. I look at the crowd. Who's bidding? I pick out a nod, an upraised

*An
Owner*

finger, a wink. Then it's over again. A man slaps a label on to some of the sold fish. So that's what it was all about! On and on he races. I begin to feel annoyed and then angry. He's rushing over five or six days of grinding work at sea and he's deciding how much the men will get for it. My father, my home, our well being and of all the other smacksmen, more or less decided so quickly by a man in a white coat!

That catch sold and labelled ready for it's new owners near or far, the auctioneer moves away. Soon I hear his bell. In a few minutes time the return on another smack's trip will be decided. I have often wondered if he ponders on this. He can fairly say, "It's my job. Somebody's got to do it" – for a nice fat commission father and the others could say.

Father often drew my attention to his special people. "Look over there", he'd say, "You know him!", pointing to a burly lumper crashing ahead with his heavily laden fish trolley. "That's "Fud" Coleman!" I never knew how he got his nickname.

*The auctioneer deciding the crew's
earnings for a six day trip*

"Fud" was the full back of the Lowestoft Town football eleven.

Those were the days when the full back was back and stayed there. One match he and his partner, Gassy Cook, under no pressure had a private game with their goal keeper. "Fud" regaled us with his tremendous lofted clearance which often landed the ball in the arms of the opposing goal keeper. He often booted it straight back.

With quite a touch of awe in his voice he said, "Look there's Bertie Bews". I saw a slow moving, elderly man of medium height, his shoulders hunched as if almost overcome by the clamour all around him. I had heard of him as one of the fabled Lowestoft Town football team which reached the final of the Amateur Cup. After their defeat they were declared professionals because some generous person settled their laundry bills!

I called father's attention to a third footballing character, young, very athletic, with a mop of black curly hair. His highly coloured cheeks came from "too much whisky", it was suggested. Dusty Miller was a Scot who came to work for the herring season. He played very effectively for The Town football team. Today he would have been very much the female supporters' "pin–up".

Smacksmen loved their grub. Father's helpings fascinated me as mother loaded his plate. I vowed, that, when I grew up I would have as much. Unfortunately now that I am, I can't. I heard of two smacksmen with appetites which made father's seem a mere snack.

Number one demolished a leg of pork, two plum duffs – each enough for the whole crew – "Oi'll leave a bit a duff", he said, "Oi want t' get over it f'r a woile".

Number two "Ole Charlie", an ancient third hand, who cycled in from Aldby, a village some ten miles away from his ship, ate at one meal – nine large herrings, seven mackerel (one or perhaps two of either would have made a good meal), two sea biscuits. He topped this up with mugs of fisherman's tea. "Then they rolled 'im up 'n down th' deck loike a bloody barrel!"

I remember a very different and a much older Dusty Miller, for his adroitness with his two dogs, "Monday" and "Nellie". He was a smack night watchman because of casual pilfering even in those days. He trebled his nightly wage in this way very cleverly.

He boarded a smack. He went below with Monday and left him "On Guard". He went to another smack. He took Nellie down below and settled her "On Guard". He made himself comfortable in the third cabin and stayed. So he watched over three smacks and earned three wages.

Dusty reminds me that most fishermen were dog lovers. Some of the dogs became as much a market character as their owners. On the whole they preferred mongrels. As Larko said, "They're more 've a dawg th'n y' pampered pedigree lap dawgs". His dog, obviously of very mixed lineage, proved as much of a character as Larko himself.

He made himself known to me as I sat in the stern of East Dean. I felt a gentle tap on my knee. I looked into the unwavering stare of lively and intelligent doggy eyes set in a tangled mass of off–white hair, spreading from his head to within a few deep black inches of his rear. A brief, intense inspection of me followed. He went below.

He soon returned with something in his mouth. He dropped this at my feet – it was the ship's

Flash shows his admiration for Larko

scrubbing brush. I heard Larko's voice, "Oi reck'n Flash loikes y'. 'E don't make frien's that easy", he said, "but when 'e do 'e gives 'm a scrubb'n brush – if 'e c'n foin one".

It was his token of friendship! "'E does th' same", he said, "if Oi leave 'm at 'ome. When Oi get back Oi oft'n fall asleep. When Oi wake up there's allus two or three scrubb'n brushes around m' feet. The neighbours allus know where t' come 'n get 'm."

One morning during a settling, Father and Skipper were in the cabin of East Dean enjoying a mug of tea and biscuits. Father offered a piece to Flash. He refused even to touch it. He turned away. Father said to skipper,

Both pipes upside down

"Doesn't Flash like biscuit or has he suddenly turned against me?" "Watch me", Larko said. He broke off a piece of biscuit – the same kind. He offered it to Flash who eagerly gobbled it up. Another piece disappeared as quickly.

"Oive trained 'im t' do this", Skipper said, "So 'e won't take anyth'n fr'm anybody 'cept me 'n th' missus". The dog before Flash died in agony, he explained, after eating a piece of poisoned meat thrown over his garden wall. "No dog a moine 'll doiy like that agin", he said.

Uncle Bob had a dog, Guidee, a mongrel, mostly Airedale. He was a one–man dog. He tolerated me, but, if I tried too hard to please him, a quick growl warned, "So far and no further". Uncle Bob failed to rid him of his hatred of water. One hint of bath and he disappeared. He disliked ships, most unusual for a trawlerman's pet. He would not even go with him to the harbour. "But", Aunt Sarah said, "he knew when his master was coming in and he was off to meet him on board". I had not seen tears in a man's eyes before, until Uncle Bob returned without Guidee. "He had something wrong with him", Auntie said, "So Uncle Bob had him put to sleep".

There was an ancient man with his ancient dog. Each looked his age. Each moved slowly and carefully. Each clenched a clay pipe with the bowl upside down. The dog walked as near as possible to his master's heel, possibly because of bad eyesight or, as I prefer, through mutual love and companionship.

A black retriever patronised his pub. The barman solemnly chalked his pint on the slate – when his master was at sea. The account was settled when they came in together for their usual beer.

We had Zulu, a most attractive spaniel–retriever cross, bought from the rabbit catcher cum-poacher in our village in Cornwall. Naturally, he loved water and swimming. When in late 1916 we returned to Lowestoft and father again fished from his home port, Zulu often went with him.

Father told me, "As we got near to the pier heads, Zulu always became excited and ran up and down the deck. As we cleared the harbour mouth and made for the trawl dock I had to hold his collar to stop him from jumping overboard. When we were far enough in I let him jump into the water". (He must have swam nearly a quarter of a mile before landing).

Not more than half an hour later, according to father's timing, Zulu was barking at our back door. He had covered nearly three miles of busy roads including a main street. He negotiated several intricate turns and twists. "I never taught him", father said.

Another market dog, a retriever, sported a unique brass studded collar with a small brass plate. Engraved on it were the initials R.A.O.B. and a number. His master was such a keen member of "The Royal and Ancient Order of the Buffaloes", that he enrolled his dog.

I must include this story of one of my supposedly "Oi c'n stand up t' anyth'n" skippers.

He came aboard. "Everything ready? We'll go", he said after changing into his sea clothes. His smack just cleared the harbour mouth and he was about to hand over to the mate when he astonished his crew. "We've gotta get back", he said, turning the smack round. "I ain't got me drops. Oi never go without 'm".

Two quacks displayed their very old cure–alls. "Good f'r evryth'n 'cept a wood'n leg". One, who was also The Punch and Judy man, went from ship to ship, and around the market with his habitual call "Oive got'm", which became his nickname. There was another, "Ole Carlton". His cure – he called his "Dutch Drops".

Mrs. Love hawked her "fabulous" ointment in little, round boxes, made, she claimed, from a family secret recipe handed directly down to her. She too insisted, "It'll cure anything".

I do not know how successful these "cure alls" were. Father, other than that attack of salt water boils, had no need for any. I do not remember even a common cold until the last year or so of his life. He complained then of the "screws", touches of rheumatism which many smacksmen

"They reckoned these would cure anything – except a wooden leg", father said

stoically accepted as the natural outcome of their work.

I also recall the last time I saw him. He had fallen and broken his hip and was in Dover hospital. The usual pneumonia followed. He showed me his hands, no longer the smacksman's. They were pale. Expertly manicured! "I'm getting soft", he said. It was the first, and last time, I heard him grumble.

Chapter 13

The 1914-18 War

It came with one of the most beautiful sunsets I have ever seen. Silhouetted black against it's purples, reds and golden orange I saw a smack. She sailed closer than usual, a sure sign that her skipper wanted a long distance "chat". Our man, Frank Martin, climbed into the shrouds and holding on with one hand, cupping his mouth with the other, he leaned perilously far over the sea.

"Any news?" he shouted, as if he expected there would be.

"Yes", bounced loudly back across the waves. "We're at war w' them there Germans ... So long!" and she swept away into the gathering dusk.

Skipper jumped to the deck and spoke to father who had appeared on hearing the shouting. He, too, did not seem surprised. They chatted for a few minutes. Skipper went below. Father followed after telling Decky to, "Turn her round".

With him concentrating on bringing Crimson Rose on to her new course I felt lonely and puzzled. There was a change of feeling on board brought about by a happening which had no meaning for me. With "Not in front of the children" of those days strictly enforced in our family, I knew nothing of the German threat. I had only heard of Germany because we were told that metal toys marked "Made in Germany" were badly put together.

I was thrilled earlier that day by battleships, large and small, hurrying to the north with volumes of heavy smoke from their many funnels trailing behind. I spoke excitedly to as many of the crew as came on deck. They told me that some were destroyers and that the biggest were battleships – but not a word about war and the Germans. So, untroubled, I went below and to bed – on a locker top – the weather so quiet and peaceful. I slept long and well.

I awoke the next morning to a bright sun creating it's usual patterns across the cabin floor. Feeling excited, for a reason which I did not understand, I hurried on deck. We were just entering harbour, a strange one. "This is not ours", I said to father at the tiller. Where was skipper? It was his job to take her in. "Where are we", I asked. "This is Yarmouth", he said.

He explained that Skipper was a Royal Navy Reservist. He had been told to report if war broke out. This explained my impression that Skipper was expecting to hear we could be at war.

"No good putting in at Lowestoft", father said, "We haven't got an R.N.R. office".

Very soon Skipper appeared on deck in his shore clothes. He spoke briefly to father. He said, "So long" to the rest of us. He climbed to the top of the quay. He walked quickly away. He never once looked back. I wondered how long it would be before I saw him again.

It was a long time. Many months later he came to our house with his wife. The Navy had sent him to a ship serving on a North Atlantic convoy, one of the very dangerous assignments. A German U–boat sank her in the North Atlantic in mid–winter. With his fellow survivors he spent many hours in an open boat before being rescued. He didn't show any signs of it.

Months later he called again. As before, he had escaped from his torpedoed cargo ship and spent days in an open boat. He said so very little and barely answered all our questions. It was hard to believe that he had been through two such terrifying and testing experiences. Neither his voice nor his manner showed any change from the Skipper Frank Martin I knew on Crimson Rose.

They sent him back to the Atlantic. The next time I saw him was after the war, he was now skipper owner of a small smack, named Crecy.

When the war came our smacksmen were immediately in the front line of the naval war. Many months passed, again because of "Not in front of the children", before I learned of the many dangers added to the smacksmens' long peace time list.

Father left for sea and came home after each trip, as usual. I went to the market and the docks, as usual. I went to school, as usual. For many months the war was there, but amazingly, it's only effect I felt was the blackout.

When Crimson Rose left harbour, on August 12th, 1914, Lowestoft was in the middle of it's holiday season and every night the sea front and the two piers, the Claremont and the South or "Penny Pier" were ablaze with light. When I returned, less than three days later there were only a few dim lights left at the harbour mouth to guide the ships.

I heard the explosions of a bomb or two at night, one fell two hundred yards or so from our school in Lovewell Road. A Zeppelin passed so close to our roof that the house shook. One Sunday morning a German aeroplane flew over our house and I ran outside intrigued by the puffs of anti–aircraft fire all around without hitting it. I also saw a Zeppelin, so huge against the tiny British aeroplane weaving over and under and around it, I almost expected to hear the buzzing of a mosquito.

I, with my young sister Norah, were staying with Granny Finch when, early one morning, tremendous explosions woke us. We were hustled downstairs and under the kitchen table. I heard shells whistling overhead. "I'm sure one clipped your chimney", I said to Granny. We learned later that it landed in the next road. In our innocence we went into the back garden! Somebody decided it was safer indoors. No sooner had Granny, in her night dress, closed the door when a piece of shrapnel crashed against it. When we saw it later, it was big enough to have cut her in halves. We heard the booming of distant guns. "That must be our fleet coming up from Harwich", we decided. I joined one or two boys picking up shell fragments; they were still warm. I learned later that German battle cruisers had shelled Lowestoft but had been driven off before they had found the correct range. Many more shells landed in the countryside beyond.

Soon the sea front and the beach were banned every night and miles of barbed wire made them impassable. Soon after a big gun and sentries were posted.

Large, grey painted steam trawlers appeared increasingly in the harbours – most had strange registration letters. All had a gun on the fore deck.

The observation balloon looked just like a huge kite

A net hung up forrard, steel for mine sweeping. Their crews looked so different, almost too neat and tidy. They all wore the naval uniform, with skippers and mates outstanding in their special naval rig out, complete with a peaked caps. Skippers were made even more resplendent by a glittering brass cap badge and twinkling brass buttons.

My first such resplendent skipper passed by our house – he was the father of a school pal. His beautifully tailored naval uniform fitted his typical smacksman's figure – "as tall as e's broad" – perfectly. His buttons twinkled. His cap badge shone beneath it's immaculate whiter than white top. His wife clung to his arm in the manner of a fan with her pop star as he strode by (strode to describe a Lowestoft skipper's walk!). I recalled him in his trawling "glad rags"!

Another strange ship, also painted Royal Navy grey, dwarfed all the others. I first saw her moored, almost filling, the herring dock. She had everything to fit my idea of a real battleship, in particular a huge gun which seemed, almost, to fill her foredeck. How could such a great ship get into our harbour? She could only have squeezed through the entrance with an inch or two spare on each side. I understood when I heard she was a "monitor", specifically designed for service on the African rivers.

Possibly even more memorable was the balloon which permanently soared above her secured by a cable. Slung below it was a large basket, regularly manned by two observers, with binoculars trained on the North Sea, looking for German submarines, battleships, aeroplanes or zeppelins. When she went to sea it went with her like a giant kite.

It was Uncle Joe, father's younger brother, who first brought the reality of war right into our home.

"He never did well at school", Granny said. I first clearly remember him as an errand boy at an off–licence. He was among my favourites, dating from the first time I saw him in the family photograph album in his football team – and he was wearing a Real Football Jersey! It was one of my early ambitions to have such a one.

I cannot remember Uncle Joe coming to our house before – he was very shy. He came to tell his big brother, father, that he had volunteered to serve on one of Lowestoft's armed smacks.

"You see, Billy", he explained, "We have our own gun. It's hidden by a dummy companion top. We carry on fish'n until a U–boat comes up. Then we drop th' dummy cabin top 'n take 'er on!". "Then", he went on to explain, "we 'ave a proper sailor's cap which we put on, 'n a white ensign to hoist up the main mast. If we didn't do that", he

added, "They could treat us like pirates!" (The exclamation mark is mine). So in the considered opinion of His Majesty's Lords of The Admiralty, with a kind of pop gun, her crew in sailor's caps, a white ensign to fly at her mast head, Uncle Bob's wooden sailing smack became a fighting ship, ready to "take on" a machine manned by a professional crew and three or four times bigger than herself. Even as a boy I could see the magnificent folly of it all. Neither of my parents attempted to dissuade him.

A month or so later Uncle Joe came again. He brought with him a complicated form and questionnaire from The Admiralty to claim compensation for the loss of his "personal effects". His smack had "taken on" a German sub, and lost. "They made us take t' th' little boat", he said, "'n then they sank 'er".

He wanted help with that form, "Can't make 'ead n' tail of it", he said.

How I wish now we had pressed Uncle Joe to tell us more about his naval battle – but he was "never was the one to talk much".

Uncle Joe proved to be in distinguished company. Author Joseph Corned volunteered for the same desperate service. He must have been much older. He first stepped onto English soil, at Lowestoft, 18th June 1878, at least thirty eight years before he joined Uncle Joe's band of heroes.

We have heard much of the epic story of another armed smack by the then dubbed His Majesty's Armed Smack "Nelson" – such an appropriate name.

On August 17th 1917, she "took on" with her three pounder an enemy submarine. A splinter from it's seventh shell passed through Skipper Crisp's neck. Mortally wounded, he ordered the mate, his son, to throw overboard the ship's papers and to abandon ship. Skipper refused to go with them. "Oime done for", he said, "throw me overboard". Isolated in their little boat in the deepening dark the survivors watched the slow death of H.M.A.S. Nelson.

They sculled and drifted throughout that night and the next day and night. The following morning they sighted a buoy. They made fast to it. They waited and waited until rescue came in the afternoon. Skipper received a posthumous Victoria Cross and his son The Distinguished Service Order.

Freddie Thorpe told me of his encounter "When Oi was cook on th' Umphrey. A sub came up, 'er captain ordered us t' abandon ship. 'E spoke English as good as me". He, too, watched the death of his ship. They drifted for hours before a steam ship picked them up, "'n d' y' know she was a Dutch

"Football" with a German mine!

ship! So Oi 'ad t' spend th' rest of th' war in an internment camp – which weren't too bad".

He also told me the story of Acacia. In 1917, with her trawl down, "a German sub. came up". Skipper cut her warp as quickly as possible. He then drove her straight at the enemy. She only just missed. What with the Germans so surprised by this, and the increasing darkness, Skipper was able "t' push 'er straight on – 'n so 'e got away".

He told me another story. "It's got a bit 've a funny soide", he said, and, I will add, courage, imagination, and no little footballing skill. "It wuz a mak'n straight f' the ship". She, too, had her trawl down. So Skipper cut away her valuable gear. He shouted to the mate, "Come w' me!", as he ran aft. "'Old me", he said as he clambered over the side and balanced on the rubbing stake, a projection a few inches wide running the length of the ship. He then "played wi' that bloody thing" until it reached the stern and floated away. "One blow against one

of them glass tubes, we would all a gorn t' glory", he said.

Skipper Stumpy James, told his own story which began, "Oid seen everyth'n was alright on top, so Oi went below t' join th' others". A few minutes later the mate said to him, "Skipper can y' 'ear someth'n a mov'n about up top". Stumpy told him not to be "so daft". Within a few minutes the mate said, "Oim certain, Skipper, there's someone a mov'n abou' up there". Stumpy went "t' go 'n 'ave a look".

"Oid nearly got t' th' top", he said, "when someone poked a bloody great gun at m' nose". He looked up and "Oi saw a German sailor who ordered me t' get on deck at th' double". He saw another armed enemy sailor and a young officer. "'E spoke t' me in perfect English. 'E told me 'e loiked us in England 'n 'e'd been t' Eton". Stumpy asked him why if he liked us so much, "'E was a goin' t' blow up m' bloody ship – 'E couldn't

104

answer that one". He ordered everybody into the little boat, and then to keep well away. "Oi 'ad t' watch 'm shell my ship until she sank – but", he said, "she didn't give in easily. I could a croiyed".

The government decided to acknowledge such encounters with an imposing, official certificate and a badge showing a red embroidered torpedo on a strip of blue cloth to be sown on to the sleeve – "loike boy scouts". Charlie Langley won so many that, "If Oi go on loike this", he said, "Oil 'ave t' 'ave another garnsey w' longer sleeves".

The war with it's horror and futility came to us only four months before it ended on November 11th, 1918. The smack Francis Robert disappeared with never a hint of how or why it happened. With her disappeared our seventeen year old friend Bob Barley, a decky with father on Crimson Rose when he worked from Padstow. He must have been under seventeen because of the "call up". Father suggested to mother that he could stay with us when the ship was in port. She agreed. In a very short time he became a great favourite. To me he was a grown up who was fun and always ready to "lark about". When father was called up and Bob served with another skipper, he regularly called in at the end of each trip with a very welcome "bit a fish".

One morning he came to the house to bid us "so long" before he set off on his next trip. He had never done this previously. He stayed much longer than he should have done. We crowded to the front gate to see him off. He reached the corner. Before he turned it, he looked back and waved. We never saw him again. Not a trace of his smack or her crew was ever found. "She mush have struck a very powerful German mine", the market decided.

With the raising of the age for the call up it is fair to say that wherever there were British mine sweepers there also was a Lowestoft fisherman.

"I could a croiyed", Stumpy said

"A posh uniform" (no "glad rags")

The German submarines had seriously cut our food supplies. So the government looked again at the men like father reserved because of his age and special circumstances – he was providing food, he had a wife and seven children, six still at school and he was certainly not in the first flush of youth. All of these mother stressed in her many letters to Their Lordships – but – he had to go. They sent him to the Dover Patrol – "The Suicide Squad"!

He moved easily into naval life. He always had high regard for authority. The censor came between him and much of what he wanted to put into his letters, but he managed to give us a fairly clear picture of naval life. He certainly reacted favourably to the discipline – when he came home on leave we found he pronounced it – dis–SIP–lin – that, I assumed, was the naval way.

Certain expressions, appealed to him:- Margarine "a sliding block of steel", all Murphy's nicknamed Spud, all Millers as Dusty and Longs as Dodgers. He was tickled by the naval "Oh! Oh!" for his smacksman's "ought–ought!" The naval way of telling the time, thirteen hours for one o'clock, twenty four hours for midnight and so on appealed and rather amused him. The "posh" voices of the officers attracted him.

"All the fishermen don't like the discipline", he wrote. They should have done because it was not more stringent than skippers less apparent style on the smacks – but – "no skipper barked at them all of the time!"

Father suggested that the Admiralty made a mistake by putting a very youthful officer to supersede a skipper. I can easily imagine toughies like Skipper Larko Lark or Skipper Stumpy James reacting to orders and advice from "a young lieutie wi' th' cradle marks still on 'is arse!" One such youthful officer commanded father's mine sweeper.

"He was too keen on dis–sip–line, especially it's timing", he said. "Just a second late meant trouble". One evening, after a particularly trying day on the Dover Patrol, he told the crew about to go on shore leave, "Back by twenty four hours – On the dot!" All returned by midnight, except two – the chief engineer – a Scot! – and his young English assistant. "I was not a bit surprised", father said, "They'd been in trouble before and if they were caught this time they'd be for it". Much too long after time father, who was the officer of the watch, heard loud voices from the quayside softened by frequent "shushes". "How I got them

An armed trawler such as father served on in the Dover Patrol

106

Straight from Woolworths!

aboard and down below without wakening that young lieutie I'll never know". He did not report them. Both culprits were effusively grateful, especially the older one. So the story ended on a high note for them – but – not for father. He lost his wallet and in it some letters, and his money drawn that morning. "It must have slipped out of my inside pocket when I leaned over the side to help Scottie aboard".

The Dover Patrol consisted of ships equally spaced in a line from Dover to Calais, hopefully, to block the passage of German U–boats and smaller surface ships to and from the Atlantic. It was a twenty four hours a day job. Spaced three hundred yards apart and around them a vast minefield they watched for and hoped to destroy the submarines compelled to surface.

The German navy mounted a massive attack on February 15th, 1918. They killed 70 men, and wounded hundreds. They sank nine ships. Admiral Keyes, our commanding officer, successfully appealed to those in harbour and the men on shore leave voluntarily to fill the gaps – and they did, the Admiral reported, "more defiant, more courageous than ever". Father could not tell us in his letters and he never spoke of it when on leave.

Fatherised!

With the war over mother's urgent letters must have goaded their Lordships. Father was quickly back to what was still a national service, providing food for people who, not so far back, were threatened by very severe shortages or, possibly, starvation.

Father was not so willing. He had enjoyed the cleaner, less demanding work, the food – and the posh uniform.

Uncle Joe and my other uncles survived the war. We thought father left the navy "without a mark to show for it". He went back to fishing, dangerous for many months because of the German floating mines and the many war time wrecks, not all of them marked.

Within a few months after he left the navy we discovered that father was not unscathed.

A tiny white spot appeared at the end of his nose. I noticed it first on a frosty day which made his rather bulbous tip a deepish purple. He just said, "Jack Frost won that one". My imagination got to work. I saw him on the bridge on a biting cold night – "muffled to the eyebrows". No muffling possible over his face leaving his nose jutting so vulnerably above his woollen scarf and balaclava. Jack Frost struck. "It doesn't hurt", he said. "I'd forgotten all about it".

"My eyes are playing up a bit", he said at the end of one trip. I imagined him again on the Dover Patrol on a similar pitch black night. At regular intervals brilliant lights burst from each of the long line of ships, powerful enough to dazzle and to hurt the eyes trying to adjust and peer intently for signs of the enemy. Suddenly they go out. The intense darkness returns. This goes on throughout the entire night watch – dazzling brightness to intense darkness many times each hour after each hour. I wonder how many of the many others said, "My eyes are playing up a bit".

Several trips later he said, "I must do something about my eyes". He did. He went to Woolworths. "Waste've money", he persisted against mother's argument that he should go to an optician. He returned. "I've tried them out on their proper card", he said. They were the typical wire framed glasses of the day with small round lenses.

To tell what followed I have to create a word, "fatherisation". Best explained by the story of "Father with Mother's Brand New Milk Saucepan".

It was her pride and joy. Her illness com-pelled him to deal with it. "Your mother's staying in bed", he said, "so I'll do the washing up". Everything went into the sink; cutlery, cups and saucers, plates and dishes – some of these were fragile glass. He lifted the large, furiously boiling kettle from the fire. He emptied the contents into the sink. I heard "crack, crack". "Don't tell mother", he said. He handed me two damaged tumblers. "Drop them in the outside dustbin".

Mother's pride and joy came last – her brand new shining metal milk saucepan. Father dealt with it successfully. That is until he came to the narrowness where the side met the bottom. He attacked the thin caked milk line with growing intensity. "The darn thing", he muttered (he never swore at home, no matter the provocation). I feared for the saucepan. I watched, fascinated, as it changed from shape to shape. He finished. He worked for a while "remoulding it". "That'll do", he said finally. "She'll never notice the difference". It never recovered fully. Such was "fatherisation".

In course of time he "fatherised" his spectacles. First a tiny crack appeared in the left lens. This grew. Then the right hand arm loosened. Finally it dropped off. He replaced it with string. By now the crack in the left lens had multiplied. It too fell away. The other lens remained in situ, but scratched. Cooky of East Dean describes father's performance.

"'E first stuck 'm on t' th' end of 'is nose. 'E 'eld 'm there with one hand so that 'e could put th' side piece over one ear. Then 'e looped th' bit a string round the other. Then 'e tilted th' 'ole thing. Do y' know", Cooky ended, "After all this to–do, 'e was a look'n over th' top of th' bloody thing!"

When replaced, after mother so decided, by a "proper pair" from the optician, "They don't owe me anything", he said of the fatherised pair. True Suffolk philosophising.

For a few years after the war Lowestoft enjoyed a well deserved prosperity. Father averaged thirty pounds each trip for a whole settling period, decid-edly a record! He came home after one trip looking rather pleased. After several questions he "admitted" that this one had reached an unprecedented eighty pounds. Mother no longer worried about Settling Days.

I heard gradually more of the damage the war had caused to the Lowestoft smacks and smacksmen. Twenty one smacks destroyed in just one month, August 1915! – ten in one day! Owner Mr. Billy Thorpe, father knew him well, lost five. Our young friend's name Robert (Bob) Barley is in the long list of victims in St. Margaret's Church.

Too soon the economic depression hit Lowestoft. A sad number of smacks stripped of everything moveable, now useless hulks, lay side by side in the harbour. Unemployed smacksmen haunted the market, among them, father.

Chapter 14

Tough

A book on Suffolk reads, "Nowhere is life more arduous", referring to farm workers. I saw an article in The Sunday Times with the headline ,"The Most Perilous Job of All". That must be mining I decided. I read the article. The most perilous of all jobs was trawling in the North Sea, my father's! Who is correct, the journalist or the author?

Osler, the journalist, chose his headline after studying the findings of a report by a commission, headed by a Professor Schilling, set up by the Board of Trade, to study the North Sea trawlermen. He focused upon the men of Grimsby, 2,469 of them, from 1959 to 1963. Grimsby at that time was one of the leaders in the easing of the trawlerman's lot.

Father in 1953 glimpsed a few of these better things. He sent me a letter from Lowestoft during his first visit since he retired in 1938. Bubbling through it is a boy like wonder over what had happened in those fifteen years.

"*You definitely must come to LT. You would certainly see a lot of changes, especially in the trawlers. They are all motors, some of them would get Crecy (a smack) and another smack inside them and lose them too. Directly the trawlers come in and tied up, the Crew are ready to jump ashore with collars and ties on. They never come back ill the ship is ready for sea, not even to get the fish out and not only that, they have 48 hours ashore. Oh Boy what a life Eh? Different when I went to sea Eh Lucky to get 12 hours. A man asked me what I missed most in LT. I told him, to see a mainsail go up, also I said the buggers wouldn't know how to set it. P.S. I saw yesterday Mr. Andrews. He told me he was 84 and he don't look a day older than 60.*" (He was the father of a school friend and like father had lived through 40 years at sea).

Behind his letter I detect a touch of the smacksman's pride in standing up to such a tough job for so many years, without the few improvements he had noticed. I can imagine him muttering "Let 'em have a trip or two on a smack" – as he wrote.

"*Wooden ships, iron men*"

110

I have that letter where a retired skipper comments on trawlermen as he saw them years later than father.

"In my day wooden ships – Iron men. Today iron ships wooden men".

Let us see how the Grimsby men fared from 1959 to 1963. Osler quotes 10,174 working days lost because of injuries from falls and slips, whilst working the gear, from falling objects and from being tumbled by waves.

He gives some astonishing statistics. Deaths among them four times more than that of coal miners, forty times greater than those working in all the different industries of England and Wales.

The statistics in the cleverly named story of the Royal National Mission to Deep Sea Fishermen, "Fish and Ships", 1981, reveal that the mortality among trawlermen has risen to ten times that of the miners and an amazing fifty three times more than in all shore based industries. The author, Stanley Pritchard, writes of trawling, "This is the toughest job in the world". It affirms Osler and almost repeats his title.

Thinking of the many improvements in safety, accommodation, equipment and working practices, as well as in size, I am at one with the man who, on looking at one of the latest modern trawlers, with added interest because her sister at sea was in danger of sinking, remarked "I can't think it's possible for a ship like her to founder". The smacksmen would also agree with him.

If father could write "Oh Boy what a life" after seeing two minor improvements, I wonder how he would react to some of these.

A comfortable cot in a private cabin, as against no privacy in a small cabin with a bunk, a locker or the cabin floor for a bed. Toilet facilities and hot and cold water replacing a bucket of sea water, the tub and torn pages of the News of the World and an equipped lavatory. Safety harness instead of the few square inches of their sea boots whilst hauling. Sorting and gutting under cover, instead of in the open – (I have a naughty feeling that the real toughies would regard these as somewhat "cissyish").

Now to the pressing of buttons and switches telling him the weather, wind direction, depth of the sea, where he is likely to catch any fish. During a recent television feature on the trawling industry I saw a modern trawler's instrument panel. It had a scaring range of buttons and switches. As I tried to understand I could hear father, Stumpy and all bursting out, "We didn't need all them gadgets. We 'ad 'm in our 'ead. We didn't do too badly with just a compass, a clock and a lead line." Their job was exactly the same as a skipper of today.

One gadget not in their heads, a ship to shore telephone, and not wanted! Nobody ever insisted upon his independence more than a Lowestoft smacksman.

Osler speaks of blood and fish guts leaving the deck dangerously slippery after gutting:-

"The deck is usually covered in blood and slime from the gutting of the fish, and the motion of these relatively small vessels in the mountainous seas is violent and irregular —— they have to work excessively long hours. Many men were clearly unfit to be at sea at all."

The smacksmen could say, "Decky saw t' all the muck with 'is buckets 've sea water 'n 'e did as well as any a them big modern 'oses". As to Ostler's "relatively small ships", quoting from father's letter – "some of them would get Crecy and another smack inside of them and lose them too".

To Ostler's lists of infected wounds which led to the loss of 1,000 days in one year and over 10,000 from various other causes, they could ask, "Wot about all that first aid ready t'and?"

Professor Schilling gives three reasons for his findings: Too long a working day. Lack of sleep. Exhaustion

Osler suggests that some lost overboard were suicides!. He suggests a medical examination before becoming a trawlerman and regular tests thereafter. Knowing my smacksmen I am sure they would say this is going a bit too far, or words to that effect.

Father was typical of the many smacksmen I knew, with his never a day at home because of any illness. Perhaps they were afraid to report it. He should have had at least one day off because of a very severe crop of salt water boils, the smacksman's winter scourge from the irritation of the wrists by the damp, rough serge lining of the oily frock. I saw his wrists and hands – throbbing lumps of agony almost obscuring his fingers.

We tried to persuade him to stay if only for one day. "I'll go down and tell the owner and the crew", I volunteered. Mother said, "Just let me call the doctor and then you can go". He refused, "My crew'll be waiting for me", he said. Aunt Sarah arrived. He allowed her to bind his wrists in flannelette bandages, "They must be red", she said. Then he went into the North Sea winter.

He must have suffered unimaginable agony – the rub of icy wet ropes, the cutting of the thin twine of the nets, gripping a fish, probably freezing, stowing the fish in between layers of ice and on and on, using those throbbing fingers.

He returned. He said nothing about his hands. They looked better. I asked him about those lovely red bandages, "They were no good", he said. "They got wet too quickly, so I tore 'em off and threw 'em overboard".

The size of the new trawlers surprised father. He could have fairly assumed that with all that extra space on deck they would be safer. Yet with all that for easier and safer movement, plus safety equipment, the number of accidents increased!

Professor Schilling's first reason for his appalling figures – "Too long a working day", Osler uses "excessively long hours". To this the smacksman could say, "Oi didn't 'ave a so called work'n day. Oi reckon mine begun as soon as I got on board and didn't finish until I left at th' end of th' trip". He had no set working hours, they were decided by the trawl, the ship and the weather, snatching whatever rest he could.

To Schilling's second reason, "Lack of sleep", I remember father saying – not complaining – after a particularly stormy trip, "I haven't had a wink of sleep for over forty eight hours", and falling asleep almost as he said it.

Father boasted, "I could sleep on a clothes line. I can sleep for a few minutes, an hour, two hours or as long as you like, and, I can wake up ready for anything". Anybody who knew the smacksmen would accept this – perhaps smiling at the clothes line.

At home father caught up on his sleep, and "got his head down" for any length of time he chose. He closed every window and every curtain. He firmly shut the door. In bed he, as firmly, wound the blankets about his head. Very quickly he was asleep, as we could hear. Once I mentioned fresh air, "I have more than enough of that stuff at sea", he said. A draught at home to him was a gale, immediately followed by, "Shut that window! (or door!)"

Schilling's third reason "Exhaustion" surely stems from the first two. The smacksmen could reply, "If th' truth b' known we didn't 'ave toime enough t' be exhausted".

Father, as mate, had to take the night watch. It began after tea and ended at breakfast the next morning. Even if up to tea time he had very little rest, he carried on after taking his full part in all the daily jobs, as well as sharing responsibilities with skipper.

I joined him one night. We tramped up and down, "Mustn't make too much noise", he said, "with those sleeping down below". Sleep was by far his greatest worry. "I must never let that happen", he said. "One night I just could not keep awake. I sang. I whistled. I spoke to myself. I even tried

running up and down, but had to remember those below. No matter what I did I still kept nodding off".

"Then I thought of an idea – I opened the big blade of my shet knife. I fixed it in the top of my oily frock with the point of the blade just below my chin. I soon knew when I began to nod off".

That quip of "iron ships, wooden men" has persisted throughout these comments on Osler's article and has led to obvious comparisons. The smacksmen faced the same problems and dangers as Schilling's trawlermen. What came to the Grimsby men happened despite their gadgets and improvements. The Lowestoft men had complete confidence in their ships and in their ability to carry out their job almost unaided come what may. With quite a touch of fatalism. It seems to me!

Such could prove dangerous. It so happened with Owen Martin, Skipper Frank Martin's young brother.

He was special to me. He was full of life, very athletic, a magnificent swimmer and kindly. He was the only one outside the family who ever bought me a birthday present – a duck in a cart, it's head waggled as the wheels turned. Father told me the story.

"Something was wrong with the main sheet block", he said. (That was the massive pulley, the largest on board, which swung from the end of the main boom). "I told Owen to deal with it". He could choose either to stand on a box on deck, in safety, or, leap on to the rail, only a few inches wide, very smooth and always wet or damp at sea. It was dangerously slippery but challenging.

"I guessed what was in his mind", father said, "So I told him not to do it". – But – Owen gave in to bravado. He leapt up and on to the rail. He balanced himself. The boom swung violently towards him. Owen was in the water. "The block must have stunned him", father said. "He wasn't trying to help himself! – and there was a nasty sea running. I shouted, "Man overboard!"

"Then", he said, "I had to fight with skipper to stop him from going over after Owen. It was getting dark and there was a nasty sea running. I didn't want to lose him as well". They sailed around in the growing dusk and rising seas for a while. "The waves swept him towards our bows. We probably drove him under – that was the last we saw of him".

"It should never have happened", father said. "He knew he was doing something wrong – and he paid for it".

One of those small, fortunately infrequent, notices appeared in the market windows, "£5 reward for the recovery of the body of ———". Owen's was not recovered.

"It should never have happened", father had said – but – there was always the unexpected.

To the hurdy girdy man it came in a moment of carelessness. Too near to the warp and he was a permanent cripple. To Grandfather Macey it was just one of those things – a cog broke. He went overboard badly injured. It came to Owen with his folly. Father fell overboard in harbour. There was somebody there to pull him out.

A smack had almost reached harbour in heavy weather. An unexpected great wave crashed her against the pier. Her mizzen mast snapped, but, it's boom fell in such a way that her crew crawled along it to safety. Another smack, Rose of Devon, in such weather made her final turn for harbour. A similar wave struck and drove her off course. She ended on the beach and within a scaringly few days was pounded to pieces. Yet another smack in such stormy, squally weather reached what skipper must have thought was safety between the two pier heads, but, an intense burst of wind drove her on to the pier head with her bow two or three steps up the concrete stairway, used in summer by holiday makers to board the pleasure boats. The storm abated momentarily. She slipped back seemingly helpless, but, amazingly, skipper still in charge took her into harbour.

Such happenings so often requiring the word "but", undoubtedly influenced a smacksman's view of survival and his attitude towards such things as the life buoy, life jackets, the ship's life boat and any attempt to get the best out of them. They also partially explained their fatalism – "If it's meant to happen, it will", which surfaced when we spoke about swimming. I was surprised how many could not.

"Woiy 'ang it out", one said, and another, "Oid rather go quickly". "I didn't bother", father said. It peeped from their replies when I asked, "Why did you become a smacksman?" "Oi don't roitly know" – "Oi kinda drifted inter it" and a third said", "The ole man made me. There wor noth'n'else".

It even lurked behind father's reply to the coroner at Owen's inquest.

"Why didn't you use the life belt?" he asked. "He'd drifted too far away for me to reach him, and when he came nearer I was afraid of hitting him".

Father not strong enough to use a life belt! I understood when I tried. First of all it was too

firmly jammed into it's bracket on the back of the companion top for me to lift it! When I freed it I found it too clumsy and heavy to carry quickly to the rail. As for aiming – impossible. I could only drop it overboard. Father, even with his tremendously more powerful hands, arms and shoulders would not find it easy to take it to the side and aim it, at speed.

It was encased in tough, coarse canvas, so frequently covered with white paint as to become hard and slippery. This enclosed several thick blocks of cork. The result? Well nigh useless. All the smacks had it. They had it for years. Nobody

Companion way – life belt jammed in!

had seen fit to improve it, or, so far as I knew, to complain. The same was true of their life saving apparatus generally.

They did not bother to have life saving drill. They so cluttered the little boat (life boat) that they had to waste precious minutes to clear it. I once saw a rocket in East Dean's dump hole where Larko left his chart. I discovered father's life jacket in the bottom of his bunk. It was heavy, cumbersome and it took several minutes to tie firmly enough it's several tapes. I never saw him take it out for practice.

So with Owen overboard, unconscious, and with the sea rising, the dusk approaching, unable to help himself, father struggling with skipper and the crew must have said secretly, "Wot th' 'ell do we do now?" There was no answer.

Their tough life was at times made even more so and more dangerous by the captains of some steamers, "a push'n a'ead regardless" especially at night. It was criminal when they ignored the light at the mast head telling them, "My trawl is down". This could – and did too often – lead to her prow cutting through the warp with the loss of a complete, costly trawl and endangering the smack and her crew. Some did this in fog. Father told me this using the word "fear" This was the first and only time I heard him use it.

He hated fog. "You can't make out shapes quick enough. You see something ahead. Is it a ship? What kind of ship? It plays tricks with sound", he said. "You'll hear one ahead. You next hear it to port or starboard? Is it the same fog horn or a different one? If it's a steamer it'll come out of the fog straight at us. If so, we'd be lucky to get out of her way".

"They're out to beat the records", father said, "or they're trying to get first to the market".

The greatly increased size of the new trawlers amazed father. Two smacks inside one and plenty of room to spare! This should have meant increased space for freer and safer movement around the deck, and minimised the danger from spars, ropes and blocks waiting to drop on their heads. Yet Osler refers to injuries from "falling objects", "Trapped by gear" – and – "knocked down by waves". "Wi' all that space! 'N all them safety gadgets?" the smacksmen could fairly ask.

To explain their reaction it will help if I enlarge upon my feelings when, from the top of the quay, I saw my first smack, Crimson Rose. She was a "tosher" (yet another mysterious smacksman's word), a smaller ship averaging 60 feet in length as against the "big smacks" 70 feet. Into her already not too adequate deck space – six feet shorter than a cricket pitch – and diminished by three sizeable openings, she packed a bewildering collection of objects.

I immediately wondered how her four men could do their work freely and safely. There was so much lying about. There were so many objects in the way of quick movement, some ready to trip the hurried and careless. There were those three dark openings almost inviting a fall.

Far aft I saw the tiller about seven feet long jutting out at an angle from the rudder post with it's height of some three feet and the opening through which it worked, it posed dangers for hasty feet.

Nearby reared the massive mizzen mast, with it's low boom.

Danger from the mizzen boom

Only two feet or so forward stood the cabin top, a solid box shape about three feet tall.

A few feet further I saw a massive block (pulley) bolted to the deck. From it ropes reached up to a similar one attached to the end of the main boom which made the mizzen one look slender and spelt danger to anybody over the five feet seven of the average smacksman.

A short distance further I saw the companion way. When open it threatened a nasty fall down the cabin steps. Nearby stood two slender iron funnels.

Too near to the companion top and those funnels for quick movement stood the massive tow post. It was solid enough to cope with the tremendous strain of the warp wound round it when the trawl was down.

Very near lay the little boat. This devoured the remaining starboard space up to the main mast. To the left of it the capstan and the large opening to the main hold occupied about half the deck space from the tow post to the main mast.

A very threatening object came next – a stout, round, metal bar stretching across the deck, less than twelve inches above it. They called it "The Horse", as potent a trap for unwary feet as ever existed. It had to be there, they told me, for the sliding block of the foresail sheet.

Forrard of the main mast, the deck, space diminishing quite quickly towards the bow, was almost entirely swallowed by the square opening to the smaller hold. From here even I had to squeeze by the butt of the bowsprit and that hauling apparatus with it's large projecting iron handle, like the one which tossed Grandfather Macey overboard.

From that already depleted deck space, the trawl, between shootings, took a lot more and left little space up to the companion way, the main block, the cabin top and the butt of the mizzen.

My first night time hauling proved how wrong were my first impressions and my fears quite silly!

Heavy footsteps, rasping of ropes, the clanking of a chain and the rattling of the capstan – but no loud voices – mingled on the deck above my head. They aroused me from deep sleep. It must have been about midnight. I hurried up the companion steps and faced a picture such as I had never seen before. It only could happen on a fishing smack. As I stepped on deck the monstrous black shape of the cod end rose and swung above the waves. I only caught a glimpse of it as the wind swept the flickering light of the two duck lamps to other parts of the picture. (Duck lamp, like several other smacksman's terms, such as stockerbait and latchet, is either their own or so changed by them that it is

entirely different from the original). It gave a fairly bright and flickering light. Despite the constant movement of the flame, one moment lighting a figure and the next plunging it into shadow or intense darkness, the men moved quietly and easily from one task to another. They did not tumble over the obstacles which had seemed so lethal.

Cooky was doing well in the darkness of the main hold. The steady movement of the warp from the capstan down to him proved that. The other men leaned confidently well over the rail grabbing and hauling in the netting. They fared as easily with the gutting, still using those razor sharp shet knives. Later Decky leaned over the rail and dashed up and down the heavy bag of fish, washing it as if it were broad daylight.

I am still puzzled that the writer on Suffolk overlooked the equally tough life of the Lowestoft smacksmen. I have some knowledge and experience of farming and fishing – both are arduous.

When father fished from Padstow during World War One the family moved to Rock. I plunged with great enthusiasm into the new life. I haunted Mr. Marshall's 100 acre farm in the village. I had a go at whatever he allowed.

I even tried ploughing – disastrously – and milking as lamentably – too much missed the bucket. I even helped to walk the cattle to Wadebridge Market ten miles away.

Mr. Marshall also had sheep, pigs and chickens. I "helped" with them all.

Harry Champion, age sixteen – to me a grown up – was his one farm worker. He was skilled at everything on the farm, he had to be or lose his job.

How long did he work? His day began long before I was up and usually ended with darkness. Then he went home to eat and later joined his friends who frequently gathered by the sea wall opposite our house. I often joined in their football and cricket. He slept at home in his own bed. He had some Sundays free.

Father "worked all the hours God sent". He had no set working day or week. He ate and slept on the job.

Harry's skills were many. Father, like Harry, had to be a jack–of–all–trades and master of all of them.

Mistakes Harry must have made. I can only remember one that was serious – and the poor sheep dog got most of the blame! His mistakes had to be very serious to be dangerous. A minor accident meant first aid by Mrs. Marshall, a very serious one a rush to the local doctor or hospital.

I remember a man on another farm with a badly cut hand. He casually reached up to the ancient rafters, just above his head. He grabbed a handful of filthy cobwebs and to my horror rubbed them into the wound – a kind of primitive penicillin I now know.

At sea a minor cut or injury could be dealt with or ignored. There were bits of first aid on board (I never met it or saw it used). Skipper had to learn the rudiments of first aid for his certificate. As for a serious accident – nothing but a slow sail home. I still shudder as I try to imagine Grandfather Macey's long and agonising journey to hospital. You can't hurry a sailing ship.

At sea any mistake was always potentially dangerous. A careless knot or the wrong one could mean a lost trawl or a man overboard. I've instanced that slack moment by decky of East Dean which put the ship and all on board into fearful danger.

I don't know how well Harry fed at home. I enjoyed many a filling meal with him on the farm, especially those wonderful Cornish pasties at hay making and harvest time (I can still hear the horses snuffling in their nose bags!) Father and his fellow smacksmen, compared to other seamen of his day, were usually well fed. Cooky was usually good, he had to be.

The famed ships biscuits stayed for trip after trip, in a white sack in the cupboard by the cabin door – forgotten until grub ran out. "Rock biscuit" would be a more appropriate name. I felt that a hammer was needed to begin the eating! They were some four inches in diameter, about three quarters of an inch thick, with creamy, orangey browney surfaces pitted with a multitude of holes – I found them easy to split into two, which made the task of reducing them for chewing much easier. They still posed a threat to the teeth! Cooky said, "Oi took 'em t'pieces, soaked 'm in water and then baked 'm until they wor crisp – not too bad they wor too". "One bloke 'e waz so 'ungry 'e up 'n ate one straight away – 'n 'e forgot t' do this" – Cooky tapped one firmly on the corner of the cabin table, out dropped one or two tiny insects. "Weev'ls" he said.

Harry could as it were "play" the weather. Father could not. He was in it and with it and, so far as possible, worked with it. He had to use it to win a living. Harry could at times sit back and let it work for him.

Harry like father was exploited, but I am sure he would spring to Mr. Marshall's defence as father did for The Owner. Harry took home some milk, eggs, vegetables, and bits of pork at pig killing and other bits and pieces. Father had his "taking home" fish and an occasional lobster and crab.

I feel justified in adding an anecdote from a long retired farm worker from his childhood in a tied Suffolk cottage.

"We allus made up t' th' shep'd at lamb'n toime", he said. "We used t' do odd jobs for 'm". The hope was that when he docked the lambs one or two tails would be his reward. "One made a lovely meal f' th' ole family".

Harry had his regular wages and a bit more at harvesting and threshing. He did not have weekly pocket money equivalent to father's stockerbait. Harry had no shares in the farm. So he did not have the share smacksman's constant spectre of being "in debt to the ship".

Townspeople created the country bumpkin; those of Lowestoft the uncouth hard swearing smacksman. Both were false.

To air his grievances the countryman could justly ask, "Why don't you come and see for yourself?" The smacksman could issue the same challenge knowing it usually could not be met. The townspeople could have visited the market and the smacks. Few, very few did. Most ignored them. As for going the sea with them!

One problem faced smacksmen always. A day away from the sea, no matter the cause, meant a days lost fishing and less money. Too many such days meant much less money. The owner possibly would meet the loss at first. The several owner–skippers, probably still in debt to the bank, would be very worried. The skippers and mates knew that at the next settling they would be in debt.

How many free days dare he expect? I can only risk a tentative answer.

If they made 50 trips a year averaging 6 days each that meant 300 days at sea. In between trips, as father said in his letter, "lucky to get 12 hours".

Round about 40 days in between trips did not mean time spent at home, or with his pals and "getting the feel of the town". Much was taken up by the smack. She needed a lot of looking after.

No wonder until I was about 12 father was a vague figure who regularly came, stayed for a few hours, and then went. Except, perhaps, at Christmas.

Another 12 must be added for the settlings. They were not all days of leisure. So much to be done on board. Father often came home almost as tired as if he had been at sea.

Even Christmas could go. A series of bad trips – and – off to sea you go. A dangerous on–shore gale could keep him at sea.

All I can "safely guess" is, that out of every 365 days a smacksman had a tiny few which he could call his own.

There was little grumbling. Their attitude, as with most of their trials, was, "Well, it's all part've th' job arter all" – often with a wry grin. Their sense of humour was never far away!

As to their dangers probably the sharpest reminder was the crack of the lifeboat rocket.

It brought father to mind and the life boat men. I pictured them, all volunteers, leaving their work, jumping on their bikes, catching a tram or, if they lived near enough, scurrying to the harbour where the life boat lay. I tried to imagine what it was like at night aroused from sleep by the shout "They're

straddled her. I saw men on board frantically hauling in something I could not make out at first. Soon it became a stout rope attached to a life belt. A figure quickly jumped into it. Men on the beach began hauling. I saw what seemed more like a helpless bundle of rags splashing through the waves. It disappeared and reappeared as it moved towards the rescuers. It came safely near and they dashed into the sea. At times the waves hid them. I saw the blanketed bundle hastened away. Well before this the life belt was at the ship and another bundle was already splashing towards safety.

Rescue from the stranded monster

running down." Onlookers often helped to push her out. Fancy jumping out of a warm bed and out into a blistering winter nor'easter! How I admired them. I still do, although their work has been eased somewhat by modern developments.

My most memorable rocket broke up a Boxing Day party. We were enjoying readings from Pickwick Papers, quickly ended by it's sudden crack, louder than usual because my friend's house was only a short walk from the coastguard station. We rushed into our overcoats and went out to face the biting cold of a sharp wind straight from the sea. In the brightly moonlit night was a large steamer on her side a hundred yards or so from the shore, a huge, stranded sea monster pounded by great waves.

I heard another crack. A rocket shot towards the ship. It fell short. Another followed quickly. It

Throughout, a tiny silhouette, seemingly insignificant against the great hulk, maintained it's station. It was the Lowestoft lifeboat – the average age of her crew approaching fifty.

I heard much about Cox'n Swan and wanted to meet him – but unfortunately never did. However, whilst sketching one of the "courts in the fishermen's village" – now destroyed to make way for a fish processing factory – two or three of the wives came out. We chatted. One said, "You've heard of my husband?" as if I must have! "I'm Mrs. Swan" – proudly. With her was Mrs. Jessie Thacker. She made fishing nets from balls of coarse twine from the age of fifteen for 25p a week. Like Skipper Osborne she said, "They were happy days".

The dangers facing lifeboatmen came home vividly to me when I heard of the Lowestoft smack, Buttercup, caught in a terrible storm off the Norfolk

Seamen's cottages, Lowestoft (now all gone)

coast. Despite this the Caister lifeboat with her twelve man crew – with a main and mizzen sails, no engine – set off. The courage and skill of those men, setting out in such a boat, knowing only too well what was facing them. A sceptic might dismiss it as foolhardy. A smack with four or five men on board was in danger. Came a mishap. She capsized. Her entire lifeboat crew were lost. This happened in 1901, four years before I was born.

The attitude of most on land to the smacksmen was not helpful. Their marked change from the man at sea showed that they felt it. The majority of those I knew adapted almost instinctively as soon as they stepped ashore. How else can I begin to explain the difference between skippers and the crews I knew on the trip and the change which began even with their shore clothes. I readily recall my near panic when I first met my sea father on Crimson Rose, as well as the pleasure of home father's return when we stepped on to the quayside at the end of the trip.

On land they had to conform with a life of which they had minimal experience and little – or no – influence, except perhaps at home.

On land, unless we so decided differently, we had as little to do with smacksmen and so were ignorant of their life at sea. It is more or less true to say that neither side did much to bridge the gap. Smacksmen and their families hardly ranked at all in the clearly marked and firmly maintained social hierarchy of Lowestoft. That I was a smacksman's son was not so much a handicap but more of a disadvantage – especially when it came to the mothers of eligible young ladies!

My conversation with a lady of the dowager class about that time reveals much.

"Where do you come from?" "Lowestoft".

"Isn't that where they fish?" "Yes".

"Aren't the fisher wives quaint!" – silence.

Mother was not amused!

Smacksmen were saddled, unfairly, with a reputation which lingered from the many years past because of "Fleeting". It still labelled them as rough, tough, hard swearing, with a few other unpleasant adjectives.

"Fleeting" meant fishing in large groups of smacks commanded, very firmly, by "The Admiral" himself a smacksman. It also meant staying at sea for weeks on end supplied by a carrier, a large steamer to which they ferried their catch which then took it to market.

Just the taking of the fish to the carrier in all weathers was trying and dangerous enough, but man–handling it up and over the tall sides on to it's deck was even more so and led to accidents and several deaths.

Living on a smack, four or five men crowded into the fusty cabin, the atmosphere stinking in bad weather with the hatches firmly closed; together with the endless labour and the exhausting and dangerous trips to the carrier beggars my imagination. No radio or television in those days. No wonder arguments, followed by blows, very soon broke out. Into this lethally explosive situation came the Dutch Copers – really floating pubs selling cheap, low quality spirits and beer.

So came drunkenness, more frequent quarrelling, more and more dangerous fighting. The stories which came ashore! Young cooks and deckhands cruelly bullied and worse. Heart rending as well as disgraceful stories were told of blasphemy, swearing, even of suicide and attempted murder.

Such is the unattractive image of the smacksmen which persisted into my day years later.

Frequently I saw a very different smack in harbour. Our men did try to make their's tidy – but she really was so. Her sails were white, their's were that deep, rich reddy brown. She had LO for London. Theirs had LT for Lowestoft. Her skipper wore a neat naval type uniform, a clerical collar and a peaked cap. Theirs wore the usual glad rags and flat cap. Both fished. I discovered that she was also a hospital and a chapel. Her Owner was The National Mission to Deep Sea Fishermen to which father paid half–a–crown each year. I came to know her skipper, he lived not far from us.

She must have reminded the older smacksmen of those terrible fleeting days which Grandfather Macey had suffered. That wonderful Christian inspired mission swept away the evil of the copers, which it was founded especially to do.

As to hard swearing. I heard it infrequently, but, as the basis of their vocabulary, never. There were the usual bloodys and buggers, but no filth or obscenity.

One decky claimed he could carry out a double boast. To haul up the mizzen by himself – usually requiring two or three men, or the capstan and swear all the time without repetition. He heaved and heaved. His face became redder and redder. He mumbled a string of words, whether it was all swearing and if he repeated himself I was too inexperienced to judge. The mizzen moved slowly and steadily up. His strength was amazing – Father came. He knew the words. He spoke to Decky so quietly I could not hear his words. Decky stopped. Father helped him to lower the mizzen without the potentially dangerous crash.

Drunkenness – I lived throughout my boyhood in the smacksman's district of South Lowestoft. I saw their pubs. I saw some drunks. We were not allowed out on Saturday evenings. If the level of drunkenness had persisted from fleeting days I would have seen all but a few smacks in harbour waiting for their crews to reel aboard.

I am not claiming that they all became non–drinkers and joined the Band of Hope! Larko came on board drunk once. Father saved him from discovery and the probable loss of his skipper's certificate. Uncle Bob "liked his pint". The family kept this a secret from his bible thumping father. Granny Macey told me that Grandfather's bankruptcy was the direct result of his becoming "an easy touch" after a glass or two of whisky.

It is only fair to confess that father was drunk – once. "Can't remember anything about it!" he insisted.

It happened just after his marriage. He was a decky. His smack, the strangely named Arbor Vita, docked after a long and stormy trip. Father, tired and hungry, was persuaded by skipper to drop in to the local before going home – a walk of four to five miles for father. He downed a small port – on an empty inexperienced stomach!

He got home – How, he never knew. Mother was not pleased. So he tried humour as he usually did when he felt he had upset her, which was rarely. He reeled down the garden. He hustled the dog out of it's kennel and took it's place. He poked his head out and barked and growled. Mother was not amused. She ran into the kitchen. She seized the large bucket of water just re–filled from the well. She emptied it over father. Fortunately for him Uncle Alf arrived. He, well experienced in such matters, took charge. He dried him, put him to bed. "I don't remember anything", father persisted.

Experience taught them, among many other valuable lessons, how far over the rail they could safely stretch as they reached for the returning trawl. How near was too near as the warp sped and coiled across the deck. It taught cooky how to deal with it during shooting and hauling. It taught skipper, where to shoot and when to haul – when to shorten or to extend the sails. It also taught him among the many other things how to find his way home. It must have drawn in the minds of everybody on board a kind of route map, invaluable in the dark, of the whereabouts of all the ropes, of the different parts of the trawl and of the many hazards scattered around the deck.

From all of these I would choose, as one of the most important, skipper's ability to get the best out of the triple alliance of the weather, the sea and the smack.

Chapter 15

Epilogue

"They've all gone", my sister Rene said with genuine regret in her voice. She was back from a holiday in Lowestoft and that was her reply to my query about the smacks. I had left my home town several years back.

I felt the same. I knew they had to go. I had almost consciously ignored the warning when I saw my first diesel smack sailing from harbour with no sail up. I even evaded it as I spent at least an hour sketching one at the yard where she had almost finished her degradation and two or three others were awaiting their turn.

When I spoke to father about the diesel and showed him the sketch, "They make an awful stink!" he said.

I remember also Cooky's contemptuous dismissal of a steam trawler as a "fat arsed ole duck". I wonder if any smacksman saw it as the beginning of the change which would sweep away his ship, himself and his way of life.

The end came quickly with the threat of the second world war. The smacks had lasted longer in Lowestoft than in any other east coast port.

Oulton Broad, linked to Lowestoft by Lake Lothing, could provide a perfect landing space for German sea planes. So a number of smacks ended their days as barriers moored in carefully chosen places to guard against just that. Stripped of everything possible they floated – still serving their home port. Some were sold to Scandinavia for years of further service.

Others, stripped down to hulks, were towed to a place so near to the Broad they could almost see their more fortunate sisters – There they were left on the mud to rot.

I end with a touch of bitterness. Lowestoft, who owed so much over so many years to her smacksmen and her smacks, did not preserve one ship as a memorial and in gratitude to those wonderful people and those wonderful ships. They must never be forgotten

That spot, where they left the smacks to rot away, was the one I knew all those years ago as a small boy wandering the banks of that same stretch of water as "a place where boats went to die".

So my memory completes a full circle.

"The place where boats go to die"

Finch

Glossary
of Smacksmen's Words and Phrases

I have used Smacksmen's words and phrases for two reasons, authenticity and vividness. These I am sure more than compensate for the bother of referring to this glossary.

During its compilation I have realised that much of the vocabulary goes back centuries and that Chaucer would have used much of it. For instance, my father when he used a firkin tub on board, or the lavatory at home, said he was going to "evacuate", pure Chaucerian! He never said tackle as we do, but "take-L", a pronunciation centuries old.

I was also fascinated by the wide variety, from the Scandinavian countries to the Mediterranean and beyond, of the sources from which so much of their working vocabulary came.

In pronunciation they emphasised and extended the first of a two syllable word, and most others, as, say, with halyard which to them was "H-A-L yd". With words of more than two syllables they economised and got rid of at least one, as with their treatment of Lowestoft, L-ow-st'f, or forecastle, – "folk-s'l".

I have also tried to imitate their dialect for the same two reasons. Here I must mention its absence when quoting my father: the explanation is simple, he had lost it! This was the result of my mother's influence, she, as the expression was, "came from a better class", so both he, and we children, were firmly trained away from it.

---

a' – used in such phrases as "a'stern", "a'cumminin", "a'goin out".

Aft – The rear part of the ship, the lands man's blunt end or back of a smack. Goes back to the 12th century.

Bark – Very old word going back to the 12th century: "a barking pit" was the leather tanning pit; "to bark" for the smacksman meant treating the sails with a proofing liquid which gave them the rich colouring, varying from tan to a deep crimson. Ramsgate smacks always seemed to have much lighter tanned sails.

Batten(s) - Strips of wood used to hold down a covering. To the smacksman "to batten down" meant to secure everything possible against a storm.

Beam - Widest part of the ship. In front of it was forrard, behind it was aft, on it a'midships. From old German word meaning a plank, recorded first in 17th century.

Below - Pronounced b-low. Short for below deck, or down in the hold, or down in the cabin. Hence "He's below" and "Oim now a'goin' b'low."

Bend - To fasten a sail to it's spar. Hence "bending the sails", fastening the sails. Meaning to hold in restraint. Old Tuetonic word. Goes back to 12th century. Also in "Fisherman's bend", a special kind of knot, one use of which was bending a rope's end to a bucket.

Bilge - The curved part of a ship's hull on each side of her keel. "Bilge water" on a smack, evil smelling, black slimy water pumped up from that area. A sure starter for sea sickness! From an old French word meaning a bulge. First recorded 1513. "a lot a' bilge" in conversation = a lot of nonsense.

Block - The lands man's pulley. (a word never used on a smack). First recorded 1622, and came from Scandinavia. A block is a good example of the highly specialised knowledge required of the experienced seaman, as it had a crown, a tail, a swallow, a score, a sheave (or shiver), a shell, a strop, and for the landsman it must be bewildering to learn that there are various blocks, each with its own name, and that one of them, a wooden one, is "stropped with grommet strops made of wire rope". Also that by using them in certain ways one can produce a fascinating "Spanish Burton", or a "Handy Billy".

Boat - To the smacksman meant "the little boat", his life and general purpose boat, (and a useful depository for odds and ends).

Bow-sprit - A very old word probably from the Dutch, used before the 12th century meaning "a pole". On a smack the powerful spar projecting forward from the starboard bow, on which was set the foresail. It was hauled in-board in harbour.

Bowline - Nothing to do, specifically, with the bow of a ship, but a very useful knot much used on the smack. You can have a running bowline or one on the bight! Goes back probably to 12th century.

Box - (ditty) wooden box, could be ornate, that is "brass bound", in which were stowed a smacksman's personal belongings. A more recent word, 1860.

Bridge - To everybody in Lowestoft, The Bridge, the one and only link between the north and south parts of the Town. During the herring season I saw many a traffic jam - my first - because to pass from the harbour to the repair yards meant opening this swing bridge. A smacksman referred to this passage as "threw bridge".

Bridle - Two ropes running one from each trawl head to link up with the trawl warp. Word in use before 12th century, meaning to pull.

Bunk - Described in the dictionary, very aptly for a smacksman, as "a box or a recess for a bed". (particularly apt is the word "box"!)

Capstan - A word almost unchanged from the 12th century. In my boyhood - steam capstan, and a blessing.

Catch - Contents of a net. Used as early as 1465. A smacksman spoke of "good catch", "a bad catch", referring to the amount and or quality of fish.

Cod-end - Cod a pre 1250 word meaning a bag, so that "end" used by the Lowestoft smacksman was superfluous. In the trawl it was the bag at its far end into which the fish swam and were trapped.

Companion - On a smack the companion was the opening which led below to the engine room and the cabin. Sometimes referred to as the hatch or the hood. The latter a reference to the shape of its superstructure. From the Dutch.

Coper - A floating pub. Dutch word, "Kooper", to buy deal, trade. Sold cheap spirits to the smacksmen, sometimes in return for fish (1836).

Crew - "The ship's company", a phrase never used by the smacksman who usually spoke of "the crew". Used way back in the 17th century and much earlier, from an old French word.

Criticism or Praise - Grudgingly given by the Lowestoft smacksmen. Examples: "Not so good" = bad or worse. "Not so dusty" = quite good, as did "fair to middlin'". "Bad weather" was unspeakable and the adjectives unprintable.

Dead Eye - Round shaped, made of elm, pierced with holes through which passed the lanyards tightening the shrouds of a smack's mizzen and main masts.

Dirty Weather - Rough, stormy, risky for trawling.

Duffel - Coarse woollen material with a thick nap. 1667. So names after Duffel, a town in Belgium. I can remember my Father wearing duffel trousers to sea when I was a young boy. By the time I was a teenager they were rarely worn by Lowestoft smacksmen.

Fender - As early as 1626 as a shortened form of defend. To a smacksman something bag like made of rope, or of cork, or old car tyres, hung over the side to fend off or protect against an obstacle like the quayside or the side of another smack.

Fish Bag - A large string net bag with a rope attached in which the freshly caught and gutted fish were washed in the sea prior to being packed in the ice pound.

Fleeting - In my Grandfather's early days at sea he "went fleeting", that is his smack joined with others to form a fleet, with its flagship and admiral, which remained together at sea for week after week, a harsh, often brutal life. Their catches were brought to market by a steam carrier. The system had ended by my childhood.

For'rd - A smacksman's version of Forward, meaning towards the bow of the smack. "Oim a' goin' for-rd!"

Goin' Out - Leaving Lowestoft for the fishing grounds.

Granny (A) - A knot. A term of contempt for one which was meant to be a reef knot, but turned out to be a granny. Could be dangerous because it could easily jam and so difficult, or impossible, in an emergency, to release quickly.

Ground Swell - Unpleasant regular rolling waves not caused by the wind (the latter can be absent). Often coming after a gale. Very trying on board a smack as she rolled and her sails flapped and the booms flopped over with a crash of their sheet blocks. (1606)

Gunwale - Pronounced "gunn'l". Top ledge of the side of the smack's side. Appearing in 1466 as gun-wale, a beam supporting the guns.

Halyard or Halliard - Haulyard, a rope for hauling up the sails on a smack, combined with the name of the sail for example, Main halyard, topsail halyard. Goes back to 12th century. Once also meant "a net for catching birds".

Hard - Two meanings. 1. As far in one direction as possible, for instance "Hard-a-port" or "Hard-t'-starboard". 2. On the hard = on the dry hard surface just beyond the water level of the harbour, for cleaning and repairs, much cheaper than the dry dock or the slipway.

Haul - Three meanings. To haul - to bring up the trawl net. The haul - contents of the net hence "a good or bad haul". Haul - in the sense of a short or long haul meaning the trawl was down for a short or a long time.

Heavy - Referring to the weather = stormy with big seas.

Horse - On a smack a stout metal bar just forrard of the main mast, stretching almost from side to side, on which slid the foresail sheet. A terrible hazard for any careless feet!

Jib - A triangular sail set on the bowsprit. In use by 1661 (may have come from the same source as gibbet - to hang). The storm jib, a smaller version, set, as its name implies, in heavy weather. "The cut o' 'is jib", - Appearance of his face, was in use by the year 1593.

Jumper - A loose, buttonless, shirt like protective garment made from tan coloured canvas. It reached well below the waist.

Jury - An emergency rig or mast or rudder, used as early as 1616. We don't know where the word originated.

Ketch - A two masted sailing ship which had its mizzen set well in from the stern. Its boom was a nuisance to the main at the tiller of the smacks, which during my boyhood were all ketch rigged. Formerly "bomb ketch", a sailing ship carrying one or two mortars for firing bombs.

Knocking Heads Together - A conference on a serious matter usually between Skipper and Mate, or with the owner.

Lash - To make fast, to bind or fasten tightly. Frequently used instead of the word "tie". Possibly from an old French word meaning to lace or tie.

Latchet - An unsolved mystery. The name for a guernet like fish which seems to be unknown outside Lowestoft. All enquiries and reference to books have failed.

Lead-line - Used for depth sounding at sea. Had other values for the smacksman. "To arm the lead", that is to grease the bottom mentioned way back in 1481. "Deeps", those measurements not marked on the line, first appeared in writing in 1769, with the word itself probably going back as far as the 12th century.

Leeward - Always pronounced Lew'wd. The side of the ship opposite to that facing the wind - the sheltered side. "A lee shore" always avoided in a storm as being the one toward which the wind and waves were driving. From a very old Norse word meaning to shelter. The fishermen spoke of a "lee-tide", that is a tide running the same way as the wind is blowing.

Main Mast - The bigger of the two masts on a smack, both this and the mizzen mast sloped markedly towards the bow, this is very rare in British sailing ships. Used before 1420 from very old French word.

Mate - Second in command of a smack, prior to my boyhood he did not need a certificate, only experience. A mate could command an under tonnage (i.e. smaller than usual) smack.

Ob (OB?) - Very strong, oily, greyish white wool used to make the long sea boot stockings.

Pack Up (to) - Furl sails, tidy the deck and make ready to go ashore.

Painter - A very old word, exact origin and age uncertain, probably 800 years. Used by smacksmen for the mooring rope in the bow of the little boat. "A lazy painter". Extraordinary name for a lighter painter to help out the real painter!

Parcel (to) - To tie canvas around a length of rope (1627).

Rake - Used by 1626 meaning "inclined from the perpendicular". The smack's masts inclined towards the bow, most unusual, as with most sailing ships the inclination was towards the stern. This forrard rake raised the end of the main boom with its massive sheet block to a height safely above that of the average smacksman.

Ratlines - Thin ropes attached horizontally across the main shrouds of a smack, so forming a rope ladder diminishing in width towards the top of the main mast. Word known by 1611 but its origin obscure.

Reef - A word direct from the vocabulary of the old Vikings. Rolling up part of the sail so reducing the area exposed to the wind. The strength of the wind can be estimated from the number of reefs, (that is separate rollings up!)
One reef - quite heavy wind.
Two reef - quite a gale.
Three reef - Something really to worry about.

Reeve - Really means to thread or to pass a rope through a block, a dead eye, a cringle etc., etc. Heard of in 1627. Origin obscure.

Rigging - This word is over three hundred years old. The smack has two kinds.
i. Standing rigging: ropes, shrouds, braces etc.; once set was not touched except to make necessary adjustments. They gave support to the mizzen and main mast, and so they spoke of the main shrouds, the mizzen shrouds and so on. A good skipper checked these very frequently, failure to do so inevitably led to trouble.
ii. Running rigging: Ropes, called sheets, to work sails, spars etc. The origin of the word rig is not definitely known but probably came from Scandinavia.

Sail - Word rarely used by the smacksman. He used the name of the sail - main, jib, and so on. When he did use it as in foresail, it was always pronounced "s'l" - fores'l, mains'l.

Scuppers - Used way back in 1485, its origin obscure. On a smack it was a narrow gap between the deck and the bulwarks to allow water to drain away rapidly.

Sea - More often than not used instead of the word wave. Hence heavy sea meant heavy or big waves. Ship a sea - meant being swamped, or nearly so, by a huge wave. The seventh was said to be the one to look out for, but, seventh from which one?.

Sheet - Rope to a smacksman! One of his most ancient words going back to and beyond the 12th century. A sheet was a rope which stretched (a word never used in this connection!) that is finally set the sail, hence "to sheet home" meant to set or stretch the sail firmly. It also referred to the lower corner of a sail.

"Shet" - Knife - I've never seen this word in print. It was probably the smacksman's word for shut-knife, one with blades which could be shut and so carried in the pocket. All smacksman had his own jealously held "shet" knife. Razor sharp it had many uses, - gutting fish, cutting twine, cutting his twist tobacco, cutting an onion or a piece of cheese, and so on. Each had its own highly individual flavour and smell!.

Shirt Bag - A white bag of linen or thin canvas used by the smacksman to carry his clothing to and from the ship. The cord or tape which drew its opening together served as a kind of handle.

Shoot - Meant casting the trawl. "Casting" never used, also the word trawl usually omitted. He would say "We shot at midnight", or "The sea was nasty so we couldn't shoot".

Shove Off - I always thought of this as a slang expression, but to my surprise it is in the dictionary, and has been used for centuries. "Lets shove off", to the smacksman meant "Lets go", that is, move away from the quayside.

Shrouds - One of the most important and stoutest parts of the standing rigging, they kept the main and mizzen masts from falling sideways.

Skipper - From very old Dutch word. A smacksman never used "The Captain", always "Skipper". Summer visitors often used "Captain" and the Skippers loved it!

Sou-Wester - An oil skin hat with a kind of peak at the front, with a long tail behind to protect the neck. Apparently of quite recent origin, the word first appeared in print in the early years of the nineteenth century.

Stays - An ancient word meaning "to keep firm", hence the ladies garment! On a smack they were part of the standing rigging, very stout ropes running forrard from both the main mast, and the main topmast to keep them from failing fore and aft.

Stem - The bows. Originally, and very confusingly meant both bow and stern.

Stern - Always pronounced "starn" - the rear part of the smack, - the "blunt end" to the land lubber. "Goin' a'starn" = sailing backwards.

Stock-a-bait (or "bate"?) - To the smacksman it meant both the fish, usually non-prime, such as whiting, weavers, and crabs, set aside to be sold, also the money received from the sale of this fish. This was divided among the crew as pocket money, generally according to rank. I have failed to discover its origin. The word "stock" can mean something set apart for a special purpose. As early as 1440 there was a word BATE a kind of slang word meaning "a part of something taken away", so perhaps the complete term, spelt stock-a-bate means, in the smacksman's sense, fish taken away from the ship's weekly stock or catch.

Tackle - Pronounced "taicle" by the smacksman. Another very old word probably from Germany. Had several meanings. To a smacksman, a block with its appropriate sheet or halyard.

Tiller - From an old French word meaning a beam., (1625). On the smack a beam fixed to the rudder head for steering. A smacksman would say "Take the tiller", not "Take the helm".

Tiller Rope - A strong rope fastened one end to the side of the smack and when the weather was bad and seas coming aboard, the other end was lashed to the tiller. Many a smacksman was saved from being swept overboard or crushed against the mizzen by this precaution. One of the very few uses of the word "rope" by our smacksmen.

Topsail - Pronounced "torps'l". Literally the sail set at the top of the mainsail and mizzen. Hence, Main-topsail, Mizzen-topsail.

Treenail - A nail of wood, of oak, very widely used in the building of wooden ships such as the smack with obvious advantages over the metal ones. They were lighter, and much more important, could not corrode. They were from one inch and upwards in diameter. Some four thousand were used on the average smack. Treenails have been used for many centuries.

Trawl - To the smacksman his fishing net. To trawl = to fish. To go trawling = to go fishing. From old Dutch word meaning drag, in use way back before the 16th century. "We shot the trawl" = we lowered the net over the side.

Twine - Smacksman's word for string.

Watch - A period of duty on deck.

Watch-Below - Period of duty, and nearly always literally spent below resting. The word watch first appeared in literature in 1585 with exactly the same meaning.

Windward - To a smacksman Wind'd. He also spoke of South'd, East'd, West'd and so on.

Worm - To worm = Binding a rope with another thinner one to make a smoother and more durable surface. (1644).

Yaw - Mentioned first in the early sixteenth century with the same meaning as given by the Lowestoft smacksman, "To move away from the correct course", usually due to bad steering, can be caused by heavy seas (1584). Nobody quite knows where this word came from.

Into the sunset – not into the future but into extinction